LIESL ALEXANDER was diagnosed as chronically mentally ill. She was kept in a locked room, and later almost murdered by another patient.

During her years in mental hospital, she repeatedly attempted suicide and became gripped by drug addiction.

Then, the miracle happened. Liesl found healing.

In the years since then she has discovered the joys of 'normal' life. Now she wants to share her experience for the benefit of all those touched by mental illness.

TO HELL AND BACK

LIESL ALEXANDER

A LION PAPERBACK

Tring · Belleville · Sydney

Published by
Lion Publishing plc
Icknield Way, Tring, Herts, England
ISBN 0 85648 860 7
Lion Publishing Corporation
10885 Textile Road, Belleville, Michigan 48111, USA
ISBN 0 85648 860 7
Albatross Books
PO Box 320, Sutherland, NSW 2232, Australia
ISBN 0 86760 627 4

First edition 1985

Printed in Great Britain by
Richard Clay (The Chaucer Press) Ltd
Bungay, Suffolk

FOREWORD

I thank God for the forbearance of my husband James, my children, Emily and Iona, my in-laws Monica and Hugh, all of whom have borne with me during this difficult year of writing.

Also without the infinite patience of my co-writer June Manwell, it would have been very difficult to write this book. I am most grateful to her, and to her husband Ray, for their help and encouragement during endless hours of painful recollections from the past. And my gratitude to June is profound, for all the time she has given.

As my stay in two mental hospitals took place some years ago, and medical and psychiatric practices have changed since then, I have deliberately not identified the hospitals. And the names of all places and people, with the exception of members of the Alexander family, have been changed to preserve their anonymity.

CONTENTS

NO ESCAPE

I must get out.

I must escape from here.

I take my chance, down the stairs, through the door. Where am I?

Through some bushes, towards a wall. Am I free now? But what is freedom?

Where shall I go? I want to get away from this despair, this hopelessness.

Perhaps if I go to a station a train will take me home.

I can hear a police siren. They're looking for me.

I'll disguise myself. But how can I disguise this despair?

I can see the station. What times do the trains go? I don't know where I'm going. If I put my head on the rails, then it would end. There's no point in going on, is there? I haven't escaped. The despair is coming with me. I can't escape from it, or from my own thoughts.

Shall I wait until it's dark? Time is going so slowly. Perhaps it has stopped. Will I have the nerve to do it? Will the train be going fast enough if it's just coming out of the station?

The futility of it all is frightening. Nobody cares. If I do it then I'll be different. They won't be able to find me, so perhaps I really will escape.

I can hear a police car again, they're coming for me.

'Come along, Liesl, just come and get in the car.'

How do they know my name? I don't know theirs.

'What were you doing sitting there by the railway line?'

'I was on my way back to the hospital.'

'We'll take you back there, then.'

I protest. I shout. I scream, but to no avail.

The pattern is familiar. Back to the hospital, through the gates, up to the front door into the building, a policeman holding firmly onto my arms, nurses taking me up to the ward, unlocking the doors, locking them again behind me.

I haven't escaped. I'm still not free. I never was free.

'The doctor wants to see you Liesl.'

'Why?'

'You must stop this, Liesl,' he says. 'You must accept that you are a long-term patient. This is your home. You are sick and you will have to stay here for many years.'

FEAR

I was born in Lahore in India, a younger twin and the fifth child of a Lieutenant-Colonel of the Welsh Regiment, then serving in India. My mother was Irish, a colonel's daughter, witty, attractive, the life and soul of her social circle.

It was the usual and accepted thing for such people to marry within the army, continuing the traditions of that familiar world. Such marriages were not always happy, but were usually preserved by those very traditions and conventions which had brought them about in the first place — preserved at any rate while the couple remained in the somewhat rarefied atmosphere which enveloped British Army life in India.

My earliest recollection is not of India, but of the flight back to England when we were about two-and-a-half years old. Helga and I were sitting at the front of the aircraft with our mother when Helga was sick, from eating too many tomatoes! I wondered whether I was going to be sick too, and if I were whether I would be able to sit on my mother's knee.

My next recollection is of being in hospital. I was only three and I could not understand why I was shut behind glass. It was years later that I learned that suspected tuberculosis was the reason for my isolation. I was allowed to see my mother and grandmother through the partition but my only contact with the rest of the family was a wave through an outside window.

I longed for the closeness and comfort of my mother. Looking back now, I can only wonder at the distress the situation must have caused her, the heartache she must have felt at having to leave me there. But at the time I could only see that while she could go home with my sisters and grandmother, I was left alone. This was my first taste of the aloneness and sense of separation from my parents which was to plague me throughout my childhood and teenage years.

At that time we were living with my mother's parents in Ireland, but shortly after my return from hospital we moved to my father's family home in Wales. My father had retired from the army but the military manner never left him. We were now his regiment, and even the cats and dogs were treated as if on parade. His voice would echo down the large entrance hall as he barked out his orders to them, swearing in mock rage when they failed to react with military promptness. At the time, I didn't see it all as a game, a mannerism which served to hide his feelings, and I was rather frightened of him. Somehow his brusqueness kept us all at arms length.

The house itself, a victorian-gothic mansion, was very big, set in an estate of about two hundred and fifty acres. It was completely hidden from the road and approached by a long back drive. By that time the front drive had become completely overgrown, as had the formal gardens. Rhododendrons and a vast colony of bamboo now guarded the driveway, and the dams of three small lakes had broken, allowing them to drain away, leaving the whole area so neglected that the original layout was no longer apparent. But my parents hung onto their inheritance, and it wasn't difficult to see why. As one approached from the back drive and turned the last bend there was the most stunning view. The house was situated halfway up a hillside with uninterrupted panoramic views over, it seemed, half of Wales. In the evening light, when the sunset bathed everything in reds and golds, and all the world was still, there seemed to be no purer sight anywhere. I loved it as my home. But despite the beauty of the house and grounds and view, and all the comfort and luxury we enjoyed, the dominant feeling throughout my childhood was fear.

I was always frightened of the house itself, especially the attic floor of some eight or nine rooms. They had been servants' quarters at one time, but now were used mainly for storage. Most of them were full of old trunks, crammed with clothes, and old furniture waiting to be repaired or restored — the accumulated debris of previous generations.

One of the rooms had been turned into a playroom for us, but even though my dolls' house and other precious toys were there, there were times when my aversion to that playroom was so strong that I just couldn't face being in it. I also had a particular fear of a lake in the grounds. My father spent much of his time in a walled garden beyond that lake, growing vegetables for the household and grapes for his home-made wine. My fear of passing the lake was strong enough to prevent me going to him there.

A sense of separation seemed to pervade much of my existence, for I was acutely aware of the separateness in my parents' lives. Different bedrooms, different churches, different interests. It seemed as though they found life much quieter if they viewed each other from a distance. And I had a very real fear of unseen sinister presences, which separated me from the rest of the family, for I sensed them but none of the others did. It was a matter of teasing and laughter — I was 'being ridiculous', 'just showing off' and was generally classed as odd. It bothered me that I was never able to reconcile their attitude with the fear I genuinely felt, but which, as a child, I could not easily explain to adults.

My fear, and an associated preoccupation with death, must have started at a very early age. I can remember my mother being seriously ill with pneumonia when we were about four. We were told to be very quiet, so as not to disturb her, and weren't allowed to see her at all for a few days. I was terrified that she'd died and that no one had told us. Of course, my fears proved to have been unfounded, and after the crisis passed we made real nuisances of ourselves bouncing on her bed while she was recuperating! But a few years later, when she had a car crash, we were again unable to see her for a few days, and the same fear that she'd died came back to me.

When I was about eight, a young girl from the village died. I remember quite clearly sitting on a style near the house thinking about it all. It was a beautiful day, just the day for picking wild strawberries. I looked up at the sky which was bright blue with just one fluffy cloud.

'If God can make such a pretty cloud, and keep it up in the sky,' I thought to myself, 'surely he can make it that people live for ever. Death is so cruel and awful, and not at all nice for the people who are left behind. And anyway, why does the sun go on shining when someone has just died?' And I thought that it would be wrong of me to enjoy wild strawberries.

With these thoughts in my head, I went to my twin sister's bedroom. My mother was there, helping Helga search for her missing slow-worm. She took one look at me and said, 'For goodness sake, put a smile on your face. Go and wash your teeth and brush your hair!'

'I'm sad because Susan has died,' I explained. Then Helga started talking about her worm again, but I wanted to ask my mother what happened when people died, and why God let them die.

'Everybody goes to heaven when they die, darling,' she tried to reassure me.

'But what's it like in heaven?' I needed to know.

'Absolutely wonderful. There couldn't possibly be a better place for Susan to be. Now go and wash your face.'

I realized then that she wasn't going to tell me any more, so I went off thinking that it must be nice to be able to be so happy about someone's death. But somehow I wasn't convinced.

3

CHILDHOOD

When we were four and a half we were sent to a private day-school, run by a highly-strung and somewhat sadistic woman. A frequent punishment for poor work or unsatisfactory behaviour was 'no lunch', and she often expressed her annoyance by giving us a clip across the ear, or tugging our hair, as well as rapping our knuckles with a ruler. We suffered it all — literally — until we were nearly eight, when the school closed down because Mrs Davies was imprisoned for ill-treating her own child.

When it all came out my mother said, 'It makes me feel ill to think what has gone on. No wonder you had headaches every Monday morning! Why on earth didn't you tell me?'

'Because Mrs Davies threatened to beat us if we told tales to our parents,' we explained. 'And she said that you would leave us at school for ever.'

'Well, I certainly wouldn't have left you. I would have taken you away before if I'd realized what was going on,' she assured us.

By comparison the teachers at our new school, which was much bigger and better run, seemed extremely kind. We enjoyed our years there.

Our childhood and teenage years were full of activities. My parents made sure that we lacked nothing, within reason, in our social lives. We had parties and barbecues, we played tennis, we swam in the sea. I drove the tractors on the farm and helped with the haymaking, drinking tea with the haymakers, and I decided then that the best thing in the world was tea from a metal churn! We had lots of animals, including horses. Perhaps my favourite was Heidi, a palomino foal. I broke her in myself, and rode her endlessly at weekends and in the holidays, only selling her many years later to buy my first car. I also had a pet lamb, called Tabitha, which my father bought me for ten shillings. Its mother had died, so I fed it from a bottle — a gin bottle — with a teat on the end.

I enjoyed all the activities, but because of my innate shyness I didn't really like the contact with other people that such activities brought. I still hated being alone in that frightening house and I couldn't understand why I felt so alone when there were usually so many people about. Apart from our immediate family, my grandparents and great-aunt had come from Ireland to live with us, and my mother, herself a lonely person I think, tended in an impulsive way to throw open her large house to many visitors.

But in spite of all these people, to me the house always had an air of emptiness, a hollowness not hidden by all the social activity.

Our large household was not without its difficulties. My grandfather had a bad heart. We were told that he might have a heart attack and die at any time, so we were very worried that if we made too much noise, we might be responsible for his death. My great-aunt was a very nervous woman, and we'd been carefully warned not to tease or upset her in any way, but this of course made us want all the more to jump out at her from behind doors or from dark corners!

It must have been when we were about nine I first realized that my mother had a problem. Her behaviour was strange, and she was unreliable. We were told that she suffered a lot from bad headaches — a legacy from her car crash, and certainly she'd had a head injury which needed stitches. But I was very suspicious, and being that sort of age, took to playing detective. In some obscure way I felt that it might be my responsibility to sort out and alleviate her headaches.

In my detective role I would offer to wash up so that I could look through the cupboards. And if I went into her room at night for comfort from my nightmares, I would at the same time note the level of the whisky in the glass next to her bed. When I kissed her I would deliberately smell her breath, and one day I found a hot water bottle full of whisky. I told my father about that but he said, in blunt army language, that it was mother's business, no concern of his. His reply upset me, but I suppose by that time the gulf between them meant that he really was hardly aware of her problem, and so not able to appreciate the extent of it, or know what to do about it.

Why she took to drink I don't know. Maybe it was the strain of domestic problems coupled with the lack of positive happiness in her marriage. At any rate she hated the country and the country life with its limited social round, which gave her little or no outlet for her many talents.

It was my mother who taught us to play chess and bridge. Helga and I would make up a 'four' with my mother and grandfather. And my great-aunt taught me to knit — a task for which she needed great perseverance and patience because I was left-handed!

My mother and grandmother also taught me to read palms. To my mother palm-reading and fortune-telling with cards or tea-cups were party games, but my grandmother, who must have been clairvoyant, was more deeply involved and took it all seriously, regaling us with incidents and examples of predictions and clairvoyance where she'd been proved correct. It was a regular entertainment with both of them. I was fascinated by it all, willingly reading visitors' palms when asked. My mother would go out of the room while I did so, then come back and read the palm herself to check whether I'd 'got it right'.

One day I read my own palm. There appeared to be a large break in my life-line. I was very concerned for I'd learned that it could only mean disease or an accident or something traumatic. But when I asked my mother to explain it to me, she refused to take the break seriously, always concentrating on 'the lovely long life-line afterwards, darling'. Of course that was a sensible answer to give a child under the circumstances, but it didn't dismiss my worries about the break.

My mother encouraged Helga and me to play telepathy games, as she felt that twins would be good at them. But we used to plan in advance what to say, so the games weren't quite real, and we didn't understand what it was all about anyway. Even so, it made me feel uneasy.

When we were about thirteen we were sent to a convent boarding school, to be educated as 'ladies'. I was never happy there. The old feeling of separation was very real and strong, and now there was the worry about my mother. Would she be all right without us there, or would she be very lonely? Would she be too drunk to look after our grandfather, or to cope with him if he did have a heart attack?

This preoccupation made me a poor pupil in performance, reflected in my reports which were of the 'could do much better if she tried' variety. I lacked concentration, was a bit of a recluse and rather anti-social. Looking back on it, I suppose I was showing some of the signs then of being emotionally disturbed. I was living in a sort of fantasy world, drifting along with an almost fatalistic attitude of unconcern for my immediate surroundings, for school, classmates and education. My concern was for my home and the people there.

It was not long before my fifteenth birthday when I had a phone call from my mother telling me that a close friend of mine had died, suddenly and tragically in an accident. I was numb with shock. At the same time my mind was racing through all the questions of why, and how did his family feel, and how were they going to cope, and how had he looked. I couldn't take the news in. Again, I was preoccupied with death.

4

NURSING

In the spring following my fifteenth birthday I had an operation on my knee, after which I had to convalesce at home. As a result I missed taking most of my O-levels, the qualifying public examination. I was taught at home by a Miss Jackson in the attic room which had been our playroom. I still found this room especially frightening and oppressive and my mind would go completely blank, much to the annoyance and frustration of Miss Jackson. I learned nothing at all during that period, or at least I was never conscious of learning anything.

I have one vivid memory from those months at home which was to mean a lot to me. I was watching television in the library with my father. I rather liked being in there with him; it was an interesting room with a secret priesthole, disguised by shelves of leather-bound books. My father had fallen asleep in his chair, and I was watching a programme about young collectors. They were interviewing a boy of around my own age about his collection of watches, which was on display in the studio. That someone so young could have such an all-absorbing interest amazed me. He described how he found bits and pieces behind jewellers' shops and in dustbins and so on. And the thing that impressed me was how calm and controlled he seemed. He wasn't nervous at all. I wondered where he lived and thought I'd like to meet him.

As I neared sixteen, the subject of a career for me was often discussed. My mother was very bothered by my lack of purpose and direction, and concerned that my choice was limited.

One morning while I was helping her make up a bed for a guest, the subject came up again. In view of my shyness and tendency to be anti-social, my mother quite naturally favoured some training which would include hostel accommodation and supervised living arrangements.

'What about catering?' she suggested. 'It would make a good career, and very useful if ever you get married. There are lots of opportunities and it could help you see the world. You could work on a ship, or you could be your own boss and do the catering for weddings and parties. You could travel and have lots of fun.'

'Oh no,' I thought. 'But what on earth can I do? I know I must get away and do something. I can't stand it here much longer.' The sentiments of most teenagers probably, which I felt very strongly at the time.

So on the spur of the moment, the thought no doubt triggered by the practical act of bedmaking, I said, 'Nursing; I'll be a nurse.'

'Oh darling, it's very hard work you know, and not all glamour,' said my mother. 'Well, it is a training, I suppose. But do choose a hospital with a medical school, then you'll meet some nice young medical students.'

I wrote to three hospitals in different parts of England, and discovered that I'd have to sit their entrance examination because of my lack of O-levels. I finally chose a big hospital in a university town, feeling that it would be a complete change of scene for me. Anyway I had happy memories of the place, having visited my brother there during his student days.

During the interview which followed the entrance exam and the usual medical examination, I was told that the rules wouldn't allow me to start nursing until I was seventeen. (I was just over sixteen at the time.) I pleaded with the matron to bend the rules, saying that things were very difficult for me at home, that I couldn't possibly go back there and wait around for months doing nothing. I really laid it on, so in the end matron said that she would think about it, but that a final decision would depend on my knee being definitely passed as fit.

The specialist assured me that my knee was fine. When I renewed my pleas to the matron, she said, 'I'm not sure that I can take you straight into preliminary training school, but as an alternative I'm prepared to take you on as an auxiliary until you turn seventeen. I'll write to let you know when to start.'

So with that promise I returned home. Not long afterwards I received a letter telling me not only that I could start at the hospital on 23 August but that I would be allowed to go straight into preliminary training. I was absolutely overjoyed, and very excited at the prospect.

My mother took me to the nurses' home. It overlooked a football ground, which meant that it was very noisy on Saturdays — a fact which we were all to find distinctly annoying later on when we were on night duty and trying to catch up on sleep!

We found our uniforms on our beds, and all of us battled to make up our first-year hats. Eventually we all met in the corridor, all with the same problem, and not quite sure what to do about it. Then someone who'd been through the same experience the year before came along and gave us a demonstration.

The first few weeks of nursing were a mixture of enjoyment and slight frustration. The freedom of being on my own in a city thrilled me. It was such a change from country life. I felt very grown up, I suppose — having a cheque book, being able to go shopping whenever I wanted, responsible for myself. The frustration arose in the preliminary-training school — bed-bathing and bandaging dummies seemed to be a waste of time. I wanted to get on with the real thing!

Because I was shy, I found it difficult to talk to the other nurses. When I couldn't think of anything else to say, I found that the subject of palmistry was a good way of starting a conversation. I think I usually tried to make a joke of it, 'Let's see your palm. Are you going to survive this course?' or something equally fatuous.

But on one occasion which I remember very vividly, I became carried away, no longer in control. I said to Lyn, a Scots girl in our group, 'In three weeks, or three days, or three hours, something tragic is going to happen to a male member of your family.'

I was immediately very scared about what I'd said. Three weeks later to the day her father died suddenly and it terrified me that I'd not really studied her hand and hadn't consciously thought about what I was saying. On a number of occasions after that I found I was saying things not of my own volition, and I didn't understand what was happening. I was rather frightened by the accuracy of my predictions, and my insight into past events. It was no longer a game, and I started getting books out of the library on the subject, thinking that perhaps that way I would find out what was going on.

Of course the more accurate my palm reading became the more people came to me, and the whole thing snowballed. I decided that I wouldn't give out the bad predictions which I often saw of the future, but would concentrate on the past and whatever good I could predict. I was reluctant to give it all up completely. It was a way of communicating with other people, and I needed that.

5

WHERE IS GOD?

During my first term of nursing I used to go to church regularly, out of a sense of duty and habit I suppose. But the services left me increasingly dissatisfied. I decided that it was all a big farce. People were just saying words into a void — there was no God. That was a pity. I wished that there might be one, because it seemed such a nice comforting idea. Perhaps this was a deep sub-conscious hope, but there was also the frustrating feeling that even if there was a God, there was absolutely no way I could possibly learn of his existence. Anyway it seemed that neither the church with its God, nor my rejection of that idea, could give me the answers to my questions and dilemmas about the nature of death.

After I'd been nursing for a few months, and during my first spell of night duty, my emotional immaturity was brought home to me — although I'm not sure that I actually recognized it at the time. One night I was momentarily on my own in the ward, due to an emergency in another ward, when an elderly patient died. Outwardly I didn't panic. I did all the right things, rang the doctor, helped to lay her out and so on. But inwardly all the stories which young nurses are always told kept going through my mind — patients sitting up on the mortuary slab and such like. I couldn't rid myself of the idea that she was still alive. It's something every young nurse has to go through sooner or later, but the fact that it happened at night and when I was on my own didn't help. It raised again all those questions about death, and the chaos that ensued.

I drifted through those first two years of nursing, going along with whatever was happening, going to parties, chatting over cups of coffee in the nurses' home. But I had no deep involvement with other nurses or anyone else.

It was about this time that I met Martin at a party. I remember it clearly, because he was rather ostentatiously wearing a large carnation in his buttonhole. I went up to him and started eating the petals, saying that I was hungry. Such behaviour was somewhat out of character for me, but it was the start of a good friendship which was a great help to me in the years that followed.

I did all that was required of me in my work, and had a genuine concern for my patients. I had no difficulties at all with the practical side of nursing, and did well in the second-year examinations.

But I can't say that I was happy. I was tired, and I disliked making the decisions which were constantly demanded of me. My fatalistic attitude governed my actions — nursing wasn't right for me, but as I'd no alternative I'd better get on with it. Emotionally, I was finding it more and more difficult to cope with the pain and the suffering and distress I saw around me, and thoughts of death became an almost constant intrusion. My search for the meaning of life and death became more and more obsessive, and no one seemed to understand me.

Soon after my second-year exams I went to see the Matron to explain how I felt.

'I think that I ought to leave nursing. I just can't take it emotionally,' I said.

She told me to sit down, and said firmly but kindly, 'You surprise me. Your exam results and the reports from the ward are very good. You clearly have the qualities of a good nurse.'

'Maybe,' I replied, 'but I don't feel that I can cope with it all.'

She tried to encourage me, and her advice was sound and sensible. 'You may find that you are an intense person, and that you over-identify with your patients. What ward are you on?'

I told her and she asked, 'When is your next change-over? Do you enjoy night duty?'

I answered her questions. But I realized that she thought I was worrying about not coping with the work, when actually I was worried about not coping with me.

I continued to think seriously about giving up nursing, but I still had no alternative career in mind, and I felt that my family could not or would not accept my explanations. I would be 'just being impossible' — as usual. I realized that I was depressed and emotionally screwed up, but there was no escape.

One day I went to the local Catholic church, thinking that perhaps a priest could explain 'death' to me. The man I spoke to recognized me as a nurse by my uniform, and so the conversation centred on his operation and the time he'd spent in hospital.

Late I turned to Tim for help, who was a very dear friend. It was a longstanding relationship, a very loyal and consistent one, certainly deeper than any other relationship I had at that time, or had ever had, with anyone. We both felt sure that one day we would marry — it was just one of those 'understood' things. I spoke to him about my depression and my feelings, but for once he didn't understand what I was really saying. He responded lightly, treating that matter as a temporary thing to be 'got over' and 'not worried about'.

I was deeply hurt by this seemingly uncaring and superficial reply. It made me even more aware of my aloneness, my separation from everyone around me. The Matron didn't seem to understand, the priest wouldn't explain, even Tim was remote. Maybe I'd just have to experience death myself to understand it — there was no other way of finding out.

I felt that no one was taking me seriously. The more superficial everyone and everything got, the more intense I became. I did think that perhaps I ought to talk about it all, try to make them understand, but it was all too much of an effort. I was very tired and had a sense of detachment.

My friends later described me at that time as 'remote', 'just staring into space'. Off-duty, apparently, I would sit alone for hours doing nothing, not even bothering to make myself coffee when I came back from the ward. I became increasingly irritated by any 'shop-talk' and would refuse to answer if anyone tried to discuss case histories with me.

I know I became very forgetful. Sometimes I couldn't even remember which ward I was on, or when my duties were. I would go to the canteen and then forget whether or not I'd eaten. And I became irrationally suspicious. I was sure that the people around me were talking about me and plotting something over their coffee.

I have a recollection of one evening sitting in my

room, leaning on my locker and wondering whether or not to switch my radio on. After a long time I did turn it on, but turned it off immediately, for the voices from the radio were conflicting with the voices in my head. I took the radio to the kitchen to get rid of it, and to get rid of the waves coming from it, so that they wouldn't interfere with my voices. When I went back into my bedroom, I knew that I had to put something in the place of the radio, so I put a mug there to catch the waves which had been left behind. Then I heard someone say something like 'I think it's Liesl's', and a nurse came into my room with my radio.

'I don't want it here. You're trying to pollute my room with the waves,' I accused her.

'Why are you so upset?' she asked. 'You must keep it in your room. It'll get stolen if you leave it in the kitchen.'

She couldn't understand that I wouldn't mind. I just wanted to get rid of it because the people on the radio were talking about me. I tried to get her to take it back to the kitchen and turn it on so that she could hear them talking and plotting about me — then she would understand.

On duty I began to lose interest in my patients. If they were in pain it was much easier not to worry than to get involved and concerned. In any case I wasn't sure that they were people any more, at least they weren't people all the time.

I was working in intensive care. We had a patient called Clive who was on a respirator. He was only young, about seventeen I think, and had been a passenger in a car which had crashed. He was severely injured, braindamaged, and it was thought he would never recover to lead a normal life. He was totally dependent on that respirator,

32

and his parents just had to sit and watch him die. It all seemed so pointless — trying to preserve a life which couldn't be preserved. I wondered whether he was aware of any discomfort, and whether he would prefer to move into the reality of death. I remember standing in the sluice room, trying to work this out. It was time to check his monitor, but did that matter if he was going to die anyway? At the same time I was very worried about automatic switching to batteries in the event of a power cut. Or maybe Clive was a battery? Then he'd be switched into the respirator, and so it wouldn't matter, would it?

A nurse came and found me there in the sluice room, tears pouring down my face. She rang matron, whose deputy came to see me.

'Are you ill?' she enquired.

I assured her that I was fine.

'Perhaps this is all too much for you. Maybe you're overtired and run down. Go and see the doctor. He can prescribe a course of vitamins for you. And then maybe we should put you on another ward. Where do you like working?'

'In theatre and casualty,' I told her. 'But I'm quite happy here. I don't want to change.'

One good thing about Intensive Care was that death never seemed to be quite so much of a shock there, and so perhaps I'd be able to understand it. Anyway it was all so futile and there was no future in anything. I was trapped. I couldn't talk, because I knew that nobody would understand that I didn't belong in my body. I wanted to scream, and I felt very aggressive, so for safety I had to shut myself within myself. But even then I couldn't be sure whether 'myself' was secure to be within.

By that time, I was so depressed that it was easier to go under. It was all getting worse, and there was no way out other than death. If I were dead there would be no more demands on me, and I'd no longer be a pressure on others. I would be out of their way.

I just had to understand about death; I had to find out myself. I knew I should write a letter explaining this, but it was impossible to reach a decision about who to write to. Probably my parents, but could I be sure of that?

I stole some barbiturates. Which veins or arteries should I slash? Did it matter?

ATTEMPTED SUICIDE

I am trapped. I can't bear it. I can't live; I must move into death. But how?

This hate for myself, my body, my feelings, my total being, is tormenting me. Death is the only escape from this despair.

Is the blade sharp enough?

If I press slowly, it hurts, so it's better to cut quickly but the skin is so tough. It hasn't started bleeding; maybe nothing's happening.

Where are my arteries?

It hurts when I press harder, but I must go deeper. What is depth? It is something still, but this isn't still. There is so much blood, it's getting in the way. It has no right to get in my way.

There are some white things — they must be tendons. Why are they white? They shouldn't be there with the red blood, because red and white mustn't mix. I must go past them quickly.

I want to die. Why is it so difficult, so painful? Why can't it just happen?

I feel so sick and faint. That is interfering with everything, but death is meant to be the interference. My emotions are interfering. The more it hurts, the more it means that I'm getting there. But I'm so confused by the pain.

My arms hurt. The pain is excruciating. I can't move because of the pain. The pain is real, but everything else is unreal. I should be dead, but

I'm alive, and the pain is moving me into another dimension. Why is there more pain now than there was before? There's physical pain as well as the despair.

Maybe I didn't want to die. Maybe I just wanted somebody to take away the despair. Would death have done that? I was meant to experience death. Why didn't they let me? I've failed, and they're making a mockery of me. It's cruel, they're only concerned about my stitches, which are an invasion. They don't care about my despair. They don't understand despair.

THE LOCKED ROOM

I woke up in the locked room.

I know now that I spent many months in that locked room. The disjointed and confused impressions of those early days took on different aspects as various treatments were tried out on me. Of course, I must have been heavily sedated at first, because of my arms if for no other reason. But as the weeks and months passed, existence became a never-ending circle of reality and unreality. The only way I can begin to convey the horror and agony of my sick and tormented mind is by giving a few examples of my thinking during that time.

It must be understood that in the nature of things I cannot have a clear and accurate recollection of the sequence of events. I was living in an alien world, drifting in and out of deeper or lesser levels of awareness. Sometimes an injection would bring peace and temporary oblivion, but at other times it would make me physically sedated but not touch the violent emotions raging frustratedly inside me. At such times I couldn't even scream.

When I did scream I was making a noise into the nothingness of my existence, but without relieving the nothingness, because there was no response. In fact it just intensified and interrupted the nothingness, because the scream had to return to me. I thought that my scream pinned me to my reality for there was almost no other sound in that room. But was I really screaming? Was I alive to scream?

The only other sound I was conscious of was that of water rushing through the pipe in the corner of the room. I was sure that it was mocking me as it went.

I can't move from this mattress; it's dangerous to move, because if I move, it will affect them. Why are they rushing through the pipe? Maybe they're chasing each other. Anyway it's very rude of them not to stop. They're so wrapped up in each other, and in too much of a hurry to communicate with me. Do they like each other? They obviously don't want to be part of me, or perhaps they're offended because I've rejected them. But I'm worried because they may be more solid than the pipe, and they're continuous and I'm not continuous. I'm observing them, so perhaps I'm influencing them. They may take revenge on me by wearing away the pipe and then they'll break into the room, and enter a futile situation where they won't be at home. I can't control the solidity. They're instigating the coming-in and I can't control getting them out. No, that pipe is not the intrusion. I am. I am a pipe.

I have to control what's going on inside me. Do I move into the pipe and risk whatever that reality is, or do I stay and accept this deliberate interference which is here to confuse and hassle me?

Often I would plan long conversations with nurses, explaining everything to them. It was important that they should understand, for instance, about my concern for the patches caused by the paint peeling off the walls.

The patches are very naked. There is nothingness in the room, and the nothingness is observing the nakedness, and the nakedness is demanding to be observed. I'm concerned about those flakes, but my concern makes their existence futile, for the patches have to be continuous in order to be complete and real. The nothingness has imposed unreality on them and made them something they don't want to be. What happens if the patches are painted over?

I'll have to cut out a square to set them free, because they don't want to be hidden. They'd be offended and that would impose unreality on them. If only I could reach them I could increase their existence, but they're too high and I can't use my arms. So I can't have a relationship with them, and I'm responsible, for that makes a demand on them to have a relationship with me. They think that they're observing reality, because they are reality, but I can't communicate with them.

The nurses were obviously crazy. They couldn't understand me at all and they seemed to mock me.

Loneliness was probably my greatest problem during all my time in hospital and the loneliness in that locked room was truly unbearable. It was tangible — in many ways the most real thing in an eternal conflict between reality and unreality. I was so alone that even thinking about my aloneness was an invasion of that state, and so it could not be questioned.

I had the feeling of being in a test-tube separated

from everything by the glass. It was very important that the test-tube be held upright, so that people observing me could look through the glass, for it would be wrong for them to look from the top. The glass divided reality from unreality, making me untouchable. I often banged my head against the door of the room, injuring myself.

As I saw it, I was banging my head against the glass which surrounded me, for if I broke it I might break the loneliness. And maybe if I did, people would see loneliness as something understandable, and be free to interpret it as they liked. If I broke the glass, I would be outside the glass and free, and the other people would be inside it. But that thought was worrying, for then I would be like them. I didn't want that; they seemed so crazy.

The loneliness wasn't even alleviated by the occasional visits of one or more of my nursing friends. Joan and Gwen have both since described the scene in that locked room as 'ghastly' and 'horrific'. They found visiting a terrifying experience.

'There was no contact at all; you weren't a person,' one of them said. 'You just lay on the mattress on the floor, unaware even of our presence. You were wan, white, a pathetic sight. You didn't communicate at all.'

Another comment was, 'You just lay there on that striped mattress, heavily sedated, in that small rectangular room. There was just a small skylight, and no furniture at all; nothing except that mattress. There wasn't even a handle on the inside of the door.'

'I honestly couldn't envisage you ever coming out of that place.'

Another emotion which bothered me during this time, and which I thought about a lot, was love. My confusion with what was real or unreal, the way my mind gave form to abstract ideas or inanimate objects and the relationships I had with them, were all typical of my thinking patterns.

There is a square in me, in my chest; there are very fine lines around it. The colour inside the square is pink, a sort of dying pink, like a hernia on the slab in an operating theatre. So the colour is dying. My body must be an interference with this because it can't be part of it. It's imperative that I look away from this square to the other square, the dark square in the corner of the room. But the room isn't square, so how can the square fit into the room? If I shift position to fit it in, I'll shift the pink square in me. I can't control my mind to hold the pink square while I worry about the others.

And I have to look at love.

Can I observe love?

I'm not sure that all the words I learned at school can express love. I can't understand it because I'm not free to move. It bothers me to have to look at love and at the dying pink. Will the dying pink die while I look at love? Will love hurt me or be angry with me? And if I scream will that make more space for love? Emotions take up space, and love and violence can't go together in the square. Love is real because it's out there in the corner of the room, and so it's more in control and has more power. It will leave me vulnerable and the loneliness will be deeper. It can't touch my body, but how can I get rid of my body? My body shouldn't be here; I should be dead. But I'm not free to be dead, because people expect me to robot through life — they call that living! And if I was dead I would be robbing them of their idea of life. I can't abandon my body. It isn't part of me, but people associate me with it. They're wrong; it's a misunderstanding. I don't want to give them the pleasure of sorting it out wrongly.

Just because they can touch my body doesn't make it into reality.

I must move this anger into the square with love, but I can't move it until I've understood it. But the negative emotions have to be moved. I'm totally responsible for fitting the positive emotions within me, and I have to release the negative emotions which disturb the positive ones for they cannot be together. I want to go mad because I can't cope with being like this.

But will I cope with being mad?

8

TREATMENT

The sound of the key turning in the lock of my door was the only other sound, apart from the pipes, which penetrated my consciousness. I hated those keys. I felt that the nurses were cowards because they had to use a bit of hollow metal to separate me from the rest of the world. I hated the way they could use them in a split second to close out everything important. But were they closing it out or closing it in?

I know that I tried to get the keys off them, that I was violent and aggressive and abusive. It didn't seem right that they could choose when to leave or to come in and they didn't respect that I had no choice.

There came a day when I was taken out of the room. Two nurses held onto my arms and made me walk along the corridor to another small room. Some garment flapped around my legs, so presumably I was still in a nightdress. The nurses sat me down on a chair, still holding me.

A doctor spoke to me: 'How are your arms?'

I think I said, 'They're perfectly all right.' But perhaps I didn't speak at all. Maybe I just thought that I'd spoken.

'Hold onto my hand,' he instructed. But I couldn't move my fingers properly.

'Try to move your fingers,' he said.

I couldn't do it. His words seemed to be coming

to me from a long distance away, or through a tube.

'The movement should be better than that,' he commented finally.

Then I was taken into a four-bedded ward.

'What am I doing here?' I wondered. 'How long will I stay here? Is this part of the plot against me? Is someone else going into 'my' room?'

After all, it had been a sort of home to me for a long time, so it wouldn't be right for anyone else to be there. That would spoil my reality.

'Did they shut the door when I walked out? Did they go back in?'

The four-bedded ward was still within a locked area; in fact there were still two locked doors between me and freedom. But at first that locked ward offered more freedom than I could cope with. I was pleased by the move, but frightened and suspicious at the same time. I became aware that there was a demand on me to relate to the other people in the room. I felt very conspicuous. I couldn't understand why I was there with such oddities. Who were these people and what were they doing there? Were they real?

I was conscious of pleasure at having more space to move around in, and of having a window in the room, even though it was barred and I was never allowed near it. I enjoyed having a bed instead of just a mattress on the floor, and I appreciated the dignity of being allowed to feed myself — when I would agree to eat, that is. We weren't given knives to use for our food, so everything had to be cut up before it was brought to us.

I had exchanged the loneliness of the locked room for something different. But the real loneliness was still there, locked inside me. In the locked room there had been no one to express my feelings to, and if I couldn't express my feelings I had no right to cry, for crying was an expression of feelings. So my sobbing had been an intrusion, a noise which hadn't been heard; it had been a tormenting thing, unhelpful. But now in the ward I was aware that the constant presence of a nurse was an invasion and a pollution of my privacy. I would sit for hours, silent, morose, uncommunicative . . . and alone.

I was generally uncooperative about most things, I think. I was sure that they were poisoning me and therefore saw eating as persecution. On occasions I would throw my food at the nurse or across the room. I was very suspicious and at the same time my head was full of strange thoughts about what I was eating and what it might do to me.

I remember one day when, perhaps because I was a bit calmer than usual, I was allowed to join the queue in the passage to collect my own food. Usually I had to sit at a table and have it brought to me, and if I was very agitated a nurse would sit with me and feed me. But this time I was in the queue.

Poor beans. They don't want to be hot. They're very uncomfortable. They want to stay cold. I must protect them from these dreadful people. It isn't right to hurt them in this way.

Someone must have taken charge of me, got me to sit down with my plate of baked beans in front of me, and somehow persuaded me to start eating — just one bean.

I mustn't eat any more. It's cruel. And anyway, which one should I choose? If I don't choose the right one, they'll all be offended, and I have no right to upset them. But the one inside me is very lonely all by itself in the dark down there. It needs another one to keep it company. But which one?

My relationship with baked beans became further complicated when I was put onto the drug Parnate. Ann, in the same ward, was also on Parnate. We were both told that we couldn't have cheese, marmite or baked beans, as these would react with the drug, with possibly fatal effects on our blood pressure.

They're jealous. They just don't want me to be friendly with the baked beans. They're trying to break that relationship, that's why they're giving me Parnate. They've no right to interfere with my concern for the beans. I'd like to eat the beans, because if what they say is true, then I might die. And I don't want to live. But I can't eat them; I don't want to hurt them.

One day Ann was having a fit. I suppose it was an automatic subconscious reaction stemming from my nursing training that made me go to her and turn her head to one side. As I did so, my finger must have slipped into her mouth just as she clenched her teeth in the throes of her fit. When the fit was over, and my finger was freed from her mouth, I had to have three stitches in it.

She did it deliberately, because she doesn't like me being friendly with the beans. She wants their friendship for herself — that's why she's on Parnate too. Now she's spoilt it all, because her teeth have caused these stitches, and so they're part of her. They don't belong in me, in my reality.

I knew that I was extremely depressed, but it didn't seem right to me that I should be locked up just because I was depressed, and I wasn't aware of any other reason for being kept there. I was taking a large number of tablets, probably about thirty a day at that time. The number obviously fluctuated according to my behaviour pattern, and according to the type of treatment I was having. I must have become quite tolerant of some of the drugs, or else they were having a minimal effect on me for some other reason, for I have a relatively clear recollection of the start of one period of narcosis treatment, and of hearing a nurse say, 'She should be "out". I'm checking with the doctor,' and then, 'Give her double dosage.'

I'd been quite glad at the prospect of the narcosis treatment. I was surprised that they'd bothered to explain it to me, but the thought of being asleep for three weeks of oblivion was rather nice. But when they said that I'd be in a darkened room, I wondered if they mean't 'locked room'.

'Will the door be locked?'

'That's up to those in charge.'

Then I panicked.

'I'm in charge. I don't trust them at all. I wish they'd take away the door handles and the key-hole. They're conning me — there's only a mattress on the floor. It's the locked room again.'

They told me that I'd feel better after three weeks of treatment. I knew that I felt quite well, that there was nothing physically wrong with me. But they weren't willing to reach inside to the real me. I didn't want to go back into that locked room.

They gave me some medicine, some pills, an injection. I started fighting them. I must have quietened down eventually. Of course I have very hazy recollections of those three weeks. I was woken up to be fed. I felt drugged.

On one occasion I staggered out of the side ward, where I was being treated, into the main room. I fell over. Why couldn't I stand up? People were screaming. I heard the sound of breaking glass. Someone had put a fist through the window. I associated the sound with me, because some time previously I'd managed to get to the window, break the glass with one fist, then push the other fist through. I remember that I'd enjoyed doing that, regretting only that the wounds hadn't been deep enough. I remember too the pain of the stitches and trying to pull my hand away and the doctor saying, 'Keep still. It's your own fault. You shouldn't have done it.'

So in my drugged state all this came back, and the breaking glass was associated with me. I was crying, sure that they'd done this to me because I'd been planning to escape, and now I wouldn't be able to run away. They'd read my mind. Would they just leave me in that side room for ever, and forget about me?'

When the narcosis treatment was over, they stopped giving me so many sleeping tablets. I wondered why, and for the first time had an inkling that I couldn't cope at all without tablets. I tried on a number of occasions to store my tablets under my tongue to save up enough for an overdose, but each time I'd feel so awful, so shaky, my mouth so dry and my emotions so agitated, that I couldn't keep it up. I knew that I couldn't manage without them; I needed them.

I continued to move backwards and forwards between the locked room and the locked ward. When I was violent and aggressive I went into the room, and then back into the ward when I was calmer and quieter. Martin, who was a regular visitor at that time, said that I was always silent. Years later he told me, 'I'd try for ages to get you to talk, but I don't believe that you were even aware of my presence.'

I would walk across the room, he said, then stop in the middle, apparently undecided about going on or coming back. Of course he didn't realize that I found visitors rather frightening, for the demand on me to communicate was a threat and an interference to the things I was trying to sort out in my mind.

I remember a visit from my mother at about that time, just as I was coming out of a period of narcosis, I think. She was sitting by my bed. I had to talk to her, but I couldn't make the effort. I knew that I had to convince her that I was all right, because I couldn't be responsible for her feeling upset that I was ill. And somehow I had to convince her that I loved her, only I wasn't sure what love was. And what was she going to say to the staff about me? What would she plan with them? I didn't trust any of them. They were persecuting me.

Another treatment which I had at various times during my stay in hospital was ECT (electro-convulsive therapy). When I was told that I was going to have it I remember thinking confusedly that they meant an ECG or an x-ray, so I asked them what was wrong with me. They talked about convulsive treatment, but I couldn't understand what they meant. Then they didn't allow me anything to eat. That really puzzled me, for usually they were trying to make me eat — they were being most inconsistent.

As we went along the corridor I heard someone ask another patient, who was being wheeled out of a room on a trolley, 'Have you got a bad headache?' Then I was taken into the room. It was totally silent. There was a man in a white coat, and I was put onto a bed next to a machine with lots of wires.

'They're going to make me into a battery,' I thought.

They gave me an injection, and put some cream on my head, and told me that I would feel a shock through my body.

'How silly! What do they know about shocks in my body? They're not in control of it.'

They put something on my head which I thought was earphones.

'I don't want it. They're doing it all wrong,' I thought. 'They don't know anything about ECGs or EEGs.'

Then something was put inside my mouth. I shook violently. I went rigid and had the sensation of a fit. I was held down onto the bed.

Then I heard a nurse saying something about a cup of tea, and did I have a headache? I didn't even know whether I had one or not.

I was thinking, 'They're animals, sadistic, not part of society. They're not bothered about my depression, about how I feel. They're only concerned about my body and my head.'

I tried to get up from the bed and run, but now it was my body not my feelings that I couldn't control. It was a strange sensation, but my only thought was relief that it was over.

Of course it wasn't really over. I had more treatment then more again. Each course of ECT consisted of six or nine weekly sessions, and I had more than one such course. But most other times I was given a general anaesthetic.

9

THE HUT

The daily routine was unbearably dull, predictable and frustrating. There was no purpose in getting up, except to act out the routine to keep the nurses happy. There was no world outside. The world was limited to that ward. It was Alice having fits; and Jean doing everything so very slowly, standing by her bed for ages, so sweet, so calm, so dreamy, always polite; and Yvonne in the side room with her fixations about the light and cleanliness and bugs.

Nothing ever happened between breakfast and the doctors' round. Then, when someone came towards the door, we would hear the keys. The jingle of the keys five paces before the door, then the sound of the key in the lock as the nurse inside moved to the door to prevent our escape. How I hated the sound of those keys and all that they signified.

We had no privacy at all, not even in the bathroom, not even in the loos. I became self-conscious about the fact that I was losing weight. Why should they be able to sit there and watch me while I washed? There were no tap handles, and we weren't allowed to have more hot water. Perhaps they thought that we would drown if they left us unsupervised.

One day I got really angry about this and bit and kicked the nurse who was with me, butting her with my head and pushing her out of the bathroom door. But I couldn't lock the door, so I leaned against it to keep her out, frightened now about what she would do to me when she got back in again.

The medicine round was an inevitable part of the routine which I resented so much, and I know that I often fought against it. The tablets were poison, part of the persecution.

'Here you are, Liesl,' the nurse might say, holding out her hand with several tablets in it.

I wouldn't move.

'Don't just sit there, take them.' she would say. But still I ignored her. 'Come on, you've got to take them. Are you listening, Liesl?'

When I persisted in my unresponsiveness, she would get help from another nurse. I'd sit still and stare at the tablets. 'They're poison,' I'd tell myself. 'Why aren't the nurses concerned about how miserable and depressed I am? Why do they want to poison me before I tell them? Do they want me to be even more depressed?'

'Did you make these tablets?' I might ask.

'No, the doctor prescribed them. They're good for you. They'll make you fell better, and look, these are just like slimming tablets.'

'How can they be good for me if I'm depressed?'

The nurse would start to put them in my mouth, one by one, holding my nose and giving me a drink. 'Swallow them, or you'll have to have an injection,' she would threaten.

Should I or shouldn't I? I spat them out onto the floor. The nurse slapped my face — she should have slapped the tablets, shouldn't she? She picked the tablets up off the floor and the whole procedure started again. In the end I'd take the tablets. Had I done the wrong thing? Perhaps she should have put the tablets on the floor in the first place.

I was very aggressive at times, and abusive. Sally, a friend I've kept in touch with from those days, said the nurses were very frightened of me. This picture was certainly borne out by one of the (male) nurses when he saw me, totally unexpectedly and without warning or introduction, when I re-visited the hospital recently. He recognized me instantly, and recalled how he'd had to come in from another ward on numerous occasions to 'sit on' me to pacify me. I remember that when they couldn't hold me down, they'd pull my hair to control me. So I would pull theirs.

One such incident took place in the chapel when we were taken to a service on Christmas Day. I was dragged along the aisle by my hair, which was long and thick. Part of me enjoyed this violence, although of course I didn't see it as violence. I saw it as breaking the pattern of predictability, and as something instigated by me, rather than as something imposed on me.

I felt that I had to get out, to escape. The routine of the keys, the locking and unlocking of the various doors that stood between me and freedom, made escape from the ward impossible. So I'd scream at the nurses, 'Let me out. I want to get out. I want to go home.'

They'd try to pacify me by saying things like, 'Yes Liesl, you can go home when you're better.'

'I want to go now. Why won't you let me go?'

'You must ask the doctor.'

The doctor would try to reason with me. 'Well, Liesl, when we're happy that you can function in society, and not be a danger to yourself and to others, of course we'll let you go.'

'Don't you realize that if you let me out, I will be all right, because then I will fit into being all right. You've created the condition of patient in me. But if I was let out of here, I wouldn't be a patient, and so that would prove that I was all right.'

Maybe I didn't say all this aloud to them; perhaps I just said it in my head. But I certainly couldn't get them to accept that I was OK — as I saw it. Looking back, I feel that if only they had held out some hope, perhaps that I could go home in a week or a month, it might have helped. But they wouldn't shift.

I recollect trying to persuade Martin on one of his visits to bring me a hacksaw to saw through the bars of the windows. The fact that our ward was on the top floor of the building didn't seem very important to me at the time! But whether I did ever ask him, or whether this was another of those planned but unexpressed conversations, I don't know. I was aware that I wouldn't be allowed to have anything sharp; even a present of a bottle of perfume was taken away.

Occupational Therapy (OT) was therefore my only hope of escape. Of course I was only taken there on my 'good days', escorted from the ward sometimes by one nurse or usually by two nurses holding firmly onto my arms. They even had to escort me to the loo, and weren't supposed to allow me to shut the door or go in alone.

One day I persuaded a nurse to wait outside, assuring her that I was all right, that I couldn't do any harm and so on. I kept talking to allay her fears, then rushed out, pushing her hard against the wash-basin. Then I ran down the corridor and climbed out through a window. What happened next is a complete blank in my mind, but somehow

I found a hut in the grounds. I remember thinking that I'd stay in the hut until the hue and cry had died down. But the hut became the locked room, the only difference being that I'd entered it voluntarily.

I can't stay here! Why isn't it locked? It's unreal, so I'll have to leave it. But if I leave here, and this is the locked room, I'm choosing to go, and I'm capable of going, so why don't the doctors allow me to leave the locked room in the hospital?

I can recall walking through some bushes and towards the road. I became aware of the traffic, something which I hadn't seen for the best part of two years.

The cars are an interference. They're criticizing me because I'm not moving. Why are they persecuting me? Why are they offended because I'm here? They're mad, chasing each other down the hill. They're chasing each other back to the pipes. Why don't they all get into one car? Then they won't persecute each other.

I wondered where I was escaping to, or from. And was I taking myself with me? Did I know who I was?

Someone came up to me and asked, 'Are you Liesl?'

'Am I? I don't know who I am. Do I have an identity?'

10

CERTIFIED

The urge to escape was strong, but my escapes always ended in much the same way. The police would pick me up — sometimes they handcuffed me if I was violent — and return me to the hospital. There I'd be sedated and put back into the locked room. After one such escape I was told that the doctor wanted to see me.

'Why do I have to go to see him?' It should be the other way round. Doctors usually came to see me. Where are they taking me?

It was a room in the locked ward, used by the psychiatrists. There were two doctors there, as well as the sister and several nurses. I wondered if they were going to tell me that my parents had died. But the sister started by telling the doctors that I'd run away again, and been found by the railway line. One doctor asked me where I'd been planning to go, which train I was getting. The other asked me what I'd been making in OT.

'I won't talk to them,' I thought. 'Then they'll think that I'm not hearing them. I wasn't going anywhere — I was going to put my head on the lines. It's nauseating to worry about OT with that in my head.'

I got confused and impatient at being there in the room.

'Hurry up and tell me,' I said.

'Well, we are telling you.'

I thought that I'd get up and go if that was all

they had to say. Then I had a great sense of fear as he spoke.

'You've got to stop this running away. It's not helping you.'

The doctor explained that I was being held 'on Section' — that is, I was certified. That meant that every time I ran away the police would be alerted and would bring me back.

'It isn't good for you to keep behaving like this. You have to learn to cope with being here.'

'But there is nothing the matter with me.'

'Yes, there is. You're sick.'

'No, I'm not!'

'Yes you are, Liesl. You're acutely depressed. We're trying to help you. The text books would say that you're paranoid. You have a severe personality disorder. Come to terms with the fact that you're a long-term patient.'

I thought, 'But I have been a long-term patient. Doesn't he realize that I've been here for ages? What is he talking about?'

'You'll have to stay here for a while,' he said.

'I'll stay here for a week.'

'No, we're talking in terms of many years. There may be patches when you'll feel more able to cope.'

I wondered whether this was such a patch.

'You'll find it easier to cope if you come to terms with it.'

What did he mean by 'coming to terms with it?' Being more sociable and co-operative? Doing things like eating and dressing and reading?

He leaned forward on the little round table and spelt it out again.

'Liesl, you're a long-term patient, and running away won't help you. The sooner you learn to accept that, the easier you'll find it to cope. We're talking in terms of many years. People who are here for a long time accept it as their home.'

I couldn't live with what he'd said. I became extremely depressed and went downhill inside. I was annoyed that I'd ever communicated with anyone at all, that I'd ever talked to Sally, Jean, the nurses, the psychiatrist. But my despair gave me the energy to make a decision, and that was something new. My decision was to get out again, and I was fired by that thought.

One day on the way to OT, the nurse escorting me stopped to speak to a friend. Sometimes we went to OT in pyjamas but this time I was dressed. The nurse's attention was distracted and she wasn't holding on to me, so I took my chance and fled. It was morning, and I remember that I consciously took a different route to make it more difficult for them to follow me.

I panicked at the traffic, for I felt that I couldn't step across something that I wasn't part of. I didn't like what I saw, but I couldn't go back, I just couldn't face that 'long-term' idea. I was trapped.

I was very weak, and my body wouldn't move as fast as I wanted it to go. I stumbled along, trying to remember roads and places, trying to convince myself that I was OK. I went into a cafe, but realized that I had no money, so left hurriedly. I saw some nurses going into a shop. I recognized the uniform and wondered whether they would end up where I was. I became incredibly depressed. I thought about suicide, but I knew that hadn't worked before, and I was afraid that another attempt would put me back in that locked room — that was even more depressing. By now, I'd been wandering around for some time and so had missed one or more doses of the various drugs which the hospital was giving me. A hippy-looking man was walking towards me. I was crying and shaking as I met him, and I said, 'Have you got any drugs?'

'What do you take?' he asked.

Oh! What do I take? I don't know. What shall I say?

'Amphetamines.'

'Meet me in the Ship cafe at 2.30,' he said.

He walked on. Did he mean it or didn't he? I had no money. Would I need money? And why did the time matter so much to him? Time never mattered to me in the hospital, but now I had a long time to wait. I decided to go and see John, a medical student friend. I hoped that he still lived in the same place, for I meant to ask him for some money.

He wasn't in, but his room was open. I helped myself to whatever cash I could find. I didn't think of it as stealing, as he'd borrowed money from me a number of times, and I was hazily aware that he hadn't repaid me. Without another thought, I made my way to the Ship cafe.

11

INTO THE DRUG SCENE

By the time I got to the cafe I was feeling really bad. There was no sign of the man, so I had some coffee. I bought some cigarettes, and asked someone at another table for a light.

'For goodness sake, keep the thing still,' he said. But I couldn't, so he had to light it for me. The hippy appeared.

'How much do you usually pay?' he asked.

Of course I couldn't say, so I replied, 'Just state your price.'

'Two shillings each.'

He gave me five black capsules — I later discovered they were black bombers.

'Do you want to meet me again tomorrow?' he asked me.

Was it because he liked me, or because of the stuff? And why was he so secretive about handing them over? Did he have people persecuting him like I did? I wondered whether I should ask him, and whether I should tell him that I had nowhere to live.

He left. I sat there with my capsules. Should I take all five together? Should I open them up and take out what was inside, like they did in the hospital sometimes? I didn't know how to go about it. Eventually I took three and left the cafe.

I walked away, feeling no better. I knew that I'd been out of the hospital for quite a long time, and felt that I should be elated because I hadn't been caught. But I worried about how I could remember to go back to meet the hippy again. Or should I go back again? I felt no better, so he'd conned me, or poisoned me!

I sat on a wall. I just couldn't go on. Then suddenly I started to feel different. I got up and walked along the wall, intrigued by the square patterns of the stones, remembering the squares in the locked room. Had anyone ever walked along this wall before? Everything was so good; there was nothing worrying me. I was full of energy, giggly, happy for the first time in ages. But I didn't want to look too closely in case it wasn't real happiness. I was on top of the world.

'I feel so good, I'll take the other two,' I thought.

I walked along by the river, looking at the people sitting there and at the people going past in boats. I was puzzled that they all seemed so miserable — it was incredible that anyone could be unhappy.

It got dark, but I wasn't tired or hungry. I wanted to write, but I had no paper or pencil, so I went back to John's rooms. Anyway, I needed some more money because I felt so good and this feeling had to last. I was floating and everything was very clear to me.

John was in bed, annoyed at being visited so late at night.

'What on earth has happened to you?' he asked. 'You're in another world.'

'No, I'm not,' I retorted. 'You are.' I asked him for some money.

'What for?' he wanted to know.

'For tomorrow.'

'Where are you living?'

'I haven't got anywhere. Can I stay here?'

He wouldn't agree. He got up and made me some coffee, then said that as it was so late I could spend that night on his sofa. But by then I didn't want to stay, I just wanted to float on. He did give me some money, for cigarettes and for something to eat, and he allowed me to help myself to some paper and a pencil.

I wandered about, then sat in an alleyway for a while. I wanted to write, but it was too dark, so I moved near some light and wrote.

Years later when I read it again I realized that I'd written a lot of rubbish. But I was very pleased with it then.

It started to get light. I was annoyed with John because he hadn't given me the right change for the cigarette machine. I began to feel depressed again. That must be because of what I'd written, I thought, because I'd expressed something and that had spoilt my reality. It was all very strange and inexplicable. I felt that I had to go back to the hospital. I was aware of my surroundings, but suddenly the focus changed. I was sinking, and I was afraid that there would be no end to the sinking. I wasn't sure whether my body was moving with me.

My mouth was very dry and I was frightened. I thought of the hippy. I felt worse now than when I'd first met him. Maybe if I had some more of those capsules, I'd feel better. Something was racing in my head. The depression demanded that I sort it out, but the words were moving through too quickly for me to do anything about it.

I went back to the Ship cafe, but realized that again I had no money. I wondered if I could just sit there without buying anything. Would the other people in the cafe see what I was feeling?

Three or four hippies came in, and asked if they could take a chair from my table.

'C-c-c-come and join me,' I stuttered. I was scared at my inability to speak clearly. I asked them if they knew my friend of the day before. They said they didn't.

'I'm waiting for some drugs,' I explained. 'He hasn't come.'

'Ssh!'

'Don't speak so loudly!'

They spoke in whispers, but I couldn't understand their need for secrecy. A girl with long brown hair was talking about injections — I assumed that she meant hospital ones and wondered what was wrong with her. I felt that they didn't mind having me with them, and that was a nice, rather unusual feeling. It surprised me that they thought I'd been taking drugs for a long time, and they talked about 'trips' as though I understood.

I couldn't explain that I didn't know about drug-taking, except for hospital drugs. I wanted to let them know that I didn't go along with drug-taking, but that I'd had to take a lot of pills because I was sick. At the same time, I was sure that they'd reject me if they knew about me.

They boasted about shoplifting — none of them had jobs. It was a different way of life, and I didn't agree with it, but I felt resentful. Why couldn't I be out of hospital and have a job or not have a job? The choice should be mine. I became very impatient and irritable. I wondered why they put up with me — the hospital certainly wouldn't have tolerated my behaviour.

'Why don't you come with us? We're going to have a joint.'

A joint meant meat or something to me — I was

puzzled. No, I wouldn't go with them. They didn't press me, just got up to go. I realized I was being left alone, so I followed. We all walked together to a house in a side street. One of them went up to the door, rang the bell four times, then walked back down the steps.

'Strange!' I thought. 'Why not just go in if you live here?'

We went down the side of the house and into the basement. It was incredibly filthy, full of rubbish. In a way I felt at home there because inside me I was all rubbish. They locked the door. That upset me.

'L-l-l-let me out,' I screamed.

They explained that the door had to be locked because they were going to have a joint. They asked me my name, but I couldn't formulate the words to answer them. I kept stuttering.

'Come on, you need something,' someone said.

I was surprised that someone had recognized that I had a need, whatever that need might be. I felt that was such a contrast with the hospital. I was given some blue tablets, and they passed around a fat 'cigarette' which they'd made. I started to feel good again. Someone asked me if I had any money.

'No, but I can get some.'

'What do you mean, "Get some"?'

'I've got some in the bank. I'll get some and come back tomorrow.'

Then I realized that I'd have to tell them where I'd come from, in case I couldn't get back. I wanted to know if they thought that I was normal. That was very important, because if they did, then I could tell the staff at the hospital, and that would prove that I was quite all right and that the hospital was wrong to keep me there. My new acquaintances assured me that I was fine, and that they would come and visit me. They didn't reject me.

Somehow I got back to Mead Park Hospital. From reception I was taken up to the ward, and the doctors were called. They told me that I'd caused a lot of trouble, and that they were very cross, but I was still wrapped in a sensation of euphoria and everything was very distant, so their anger didn't touch me.

I don't know how long this phase lasted. I took the blue tablets I had one at a time — to eke them out. One of the other patients commented that I was a lot better. Sally said that I was very manic, and I wondered whether I should tell her about the drugs. She was a person who had a great impact on me. She was plump and always seemed cheerful, so I envied her because she was so 'happy'. She'd try to cheer me up when I was crying, as I often did. 'I didn't think anyone could have had so many tears in them,' she said in a letter recently.

My 'improvement' gained me a little more freedom. A further course of ECT was cancelled, and I was allowed to go to OT in the company of one or two other people and a nurse, instead of having to have my own escort. I worried about how to get hold of more drugs, for I realized that as long as I could get drugs I would have relatively more freedom, for the drugs were confusing and disguising the symptoms of my mental problems. I must have seemed less depressed, and the doctors probably read my increased energy, my smiling and talking, as improvement. I decided that I felt like a ping-pong ball which made everyone happy when it bounced onto the table.

Without a supply of drugs, I would seem to

deteriorate, and that would mean more ECT, more narcosis.

Pete, one of the group that I'd met in the cafe, came to see me. The locking of the doors horrified him and he kept talking about it. I got very cross with him, and tried to explain that I wasn't allowed out but that I wanted some more stuff — anything. He asked me for money. I was very excited because I'd recently received some as a gift. But I wondered whether I should give it to him; perhaps I should try to meet him and pay him then. In the end I gave him the money, but he didn't come back.

So I escaped again, from OT as usual. I intended to find Pete, but first I went to the bank, telling them that I'd lost my cheque book.

To my surprise, they accepted my story and gave me a counter cheque. I gave the nurses' home as my address, and withdrew all that I had in my account — eleven pounds and some odd pence.

The teller held out the money to me, but I just stood there. I couldn't take it; it wasn't a complete round figure. It bothered me that he didn't understand. He just said, 'Next please.'

Was he paying me this money to go away? And was it really my money? How did he know it was? After all, he'd simply put his hand into the pile of money and taken some out, so he couldn't be sure that it was mine. The paper in my hand now hadn't changed anything; it was just an interference.

I found my way back to that squalid basement. I got some more junk, but have no recollection of getting back to the hospital on that occasion, or of my reception when I got there.

12

BROOKLANDS

'Liesl, why are you so locked up in yourself? Are you not able to talk? There must be something you want to say.'

Psychotherapy was the next main event in my life when I was moved to Brooklands Hospital. Looking back, I can see that Mead Park felt that they could do no more with me. At the same time, they saw what they wanted to see — an improvement in my condition, due to the treatment they had given me. In other words, they were either unaware of my black-market drug-taking, or turning a blind eye to it and the effect it was having.

Although I was still held under the restraint of 'Section', Brooklands meant a rather different life for me. I had a room of my own, which was not locked. We were fairly free to wander around our part of the hospital, and even to go to the coffee shop in the grounds. I was allowed to have some money, and to write letters — which I did, asking for more money! I smoked a lot at that time, rolling my own. If I was shaking too much, I'd get another patient to roll them for me.

I was even allowed to go into town occasionally, if I said where I was going. That made it easy for me to keep myself supplied with drugs. I also used these outings to try to sell one or more of my paintings, for this was my source of money for the drugs. At other times I sold pictures within the hospital, to the staff and to visitors.

One day one of the consultants asked me to do a painting for him.

'Liesl, I wonder if you would do a picture for us. My wife and I are leaving here soon.'

I didn't answer.

'She's fond of blues and pale colours, so would you do something on those lines?'

I still didn't answer.

'Liesl, I'm commissioning you to do this for me. Don't you understand?'

'I can't paint well,' I said. Did he really like my pictures, or was this just his method of keeping me in hospital?

'I'm expecting an answer, Liesl. Why are you so locked up in yourself?'

'I'm not locked up,' I raged at him. 'Do you know what that means: locked up. Do you think that you are the key to unlock me?'

I wondered what I would do if he was a key. I was so angry and frustrated that I'd probably beat him up. Then he got irritated with me.

'This is getting nowhere,' he said. 'It looks as though we'll have to change your drugs.'

A nurse came in then, and he said that he would see me in one of the side rooms to talk about what tablets I should have.

'Why do they want me to talk?' I asked myself. 'If I open my mouth, that will give them a licence to do something, and I do want them to help me, so I must keep quiet. But there's nothing wrong with me, so does it matter?'

They gave me more tablets, different ones. I was sure that they were trying to poison me again. It wasn't that I minded so much taking the poison, but I objected to the fact that someone else was poisoning me. That meant that my freedom was being taken away along with my personality and my being. Part of me didn't want to die, but at the same time I felt that I had a mission to complete, and that gave me an incentive to die.

Group therapy sessions filled most of our mornings at Brooklands. We had quite a mixed bag in our group — criminals, a murderer, a man who thought he was Julius Caesar, drug addicts, homosexuals. We'd all sit in the main room of our wing of the hospital, in two roughly circular rows, twenty or thirty of us in all.

The conversation was vague and for the most part undirected. I usually sat at the back in a sort of corner where I was half hidden by the wall. I'd never talk if I could possibly avoid it, but then someone would nag at me, provoke me. They tried to create a situation where I would talk. But I knew that if I said anything, they'd get it wrong; they wouldn't understand, and they'd use what I'd said to persecute me and to provoke the others. The other thing they didn't understand was that if I turned my attention from one thing to another, it caused conflict. For instance, if I was observing the wall, and they distracted my attention from it, the wall would be offended, for I could not concentrate on two things at the same time. This conflict bothered and agitated me.

I wasn't communicating at all, and was very depressed. I felt that something was impelling me towards suicide. It had dawned on me that blackness and despair were my lot in life, and I wished that I'd never been born. I was frustrated at not being able to shift from my negative position; everything was so futile. I discovered that Maggie had somehow or other got lots of Carbutal, which she was hiding in her locker. I was meant to be at group therapy, but I went instead to Maggie's room, took all her tablets and got into bed. I examined the tablets before I swallowed them, for it was very important that they went down the correct way. They were black and white, and the black part of them had to touch the black part of me, because they wouldn't work if they went the other way. It was puzzling that the white and black parts of the tablets could touch each other, because surely the white and black parts in me couldn't be together?

The next thing that I remember is being in hospital in a cot-sided bed with two drips, one bandaged to each arm. I was very agitated and noisy, thinking that I'd died, and that the drips were taking the life out of me, moving it into something else.

I was taken back to Brooklands, but everyone was talking about me. I was put into a side ward with no furniture. There was a nurse sitting there. She asked me where I'd got the tablets, saying that they were all very concerned. But I wouldn't tell her. She told me that they'd had to pump my stomach out twice, and threatened that I'd be sent back to Mead Park if I ever did anything like that again.

For me that was the end. In group therapy after that, I just switched off. Sometimes I refused to go at all, and that would cause more upset. I was verbally aggressive, shouting at the nurses.

'No, I'm not going to group therapy.'

'Yes you are, Liesl. You can't be trusted on your own.'

'I can be trusted on my own.'

'You're coming with me.'

'No, I'm going to see Bernice this morning.'

'Well, Bernice is coming to group therapy this morning.' The nurse tried to persuade me. She took hold of my arm, and I struggled to get away.

'What does it matter to you anyway?' I shouted. 'Group — some group! Therapy — some therapy! This place doesn't do any good. Is it a place? Do you know what a place is?'

She tried to drag me along.

'No, I'm not coming,' I insisted, and picked up a chair and hurled it at her, screaming all the time.

Other nurses came to help her, and a patient walked past, saying quite calmly, 'Oh, I thought it must be you, Liesl. Aren't you meant to be with us?'

'Don't you start telling me what I'm meant to be,' I yelled. 'It's meant to be peace. But all of you are in pieces. I hate you! I hate you!'

Eventually the nurses got me to group therapy. Someone tried to draw me out by saying, 'Liesl is causing a disturbance this morning. What's it all about? Can you explain, Liesl?'

'I hate you! I hate you!' was all I would say.

'Are you feeling disturbed, Liesl?' was the calm rejoinder.

I shouted more abuse and obscenities at them all.

Then someone suggested, 'Perhaps Liesl didn't have her tablets this morning?'

'Don't direct the question to me,' said the consultant. 'Ask Liesl.'

'Drugs, drugs, drugs, that's all you can talk about.'

'Are you still feeling disturbed, Liesl?' came the next question.

'Disturbed, disturbed! You're the ones who are disturbed!'

Somehow the session eventually ended.

At some time after that I know that more treatment was mentioned, and I suppose that I slipped back into a paranoid state, although of course I didn't understand that at the time. People have since said that I was obviously very unhappy, very uncommunicative.

When I was transferred back to Mead Park that was the last straw; I was going to commit suicide properly this time, whatever it cost me. I was going to store up my tablets for a real overdose, no matter how awful I felt in the meantime. By now, my despair was the overriding emotion. There was no hope for me, no way out of this blackness and depression, except death.

13

A WAY OUT?

I was driven by my despair to find a way to end my life, once and for all.

A friend came to visit me at Mead Park and I asked him to tell Nick and Chris that I would like to see them. They were two junkie friends who'd been trying to persuade me to join them in 'pushing' to make money. My targets were to be the addicts in the clinic attached to the hospital. I'd been very uncertain about this. I had always hated the drug scene, despite my own involvement, and thoroughly disapproved of it.

When Nick and Chris came, they thought that I'd come to a decision about 'pushing'. I had indeed come to a decision — that I wouldn't do it. I was totally against the idea and wished I'd never taken any drugs. But what I actually told them was that I agreed with their scheme, on condition that they met me first with a certain quantity of drugs. My intention was to take them all myself, knowing that it would be sufficient to finish me off properly this time. So I arranged a time and place to meet them.

Once more I escaped, knowing now that I had a drug problem which I couldn't live with, that Brooklands had said that they wouldn't have me back, that if I did get caught, or if I didn't succeed in this suicide attempt, I would be back in that locked room. There was nowhere to go; I was at the bottom. Despair was so deep that I couldn't engage my mind to recognize it as a feeling. Even death wasn't really a solution, because that involved doing something; it required energy. To me it seemed futile even to put one foot in front of the other.

It was a damp day, and I was cold, clad only in a T-shirt and jeans. I'd sold everything else I possessed. I was physically a wreck, overwhelmed by helplessness and despair.

I walked onto a roundabout, but I couldn't get off it because it was round and there was no exit out of a circle. My private hell was a circle, and I could find no exit from that. I was trapped in it, going endlessly round and round with the violence and rage and confusion.

Somehow I made my way into the centre of town. I walked past a Post Office. There were people posting letters. They were all talking about me, they'd written letters about me. What had they said in the letters? I knew that they didn't care, that they only brushed past me to contaminate me. I was totally unloved. I didn't even care about myself, but I needed someone to care that I didn't care. I was so angry with life that I had to end it.

Suddenly I heard the sound of singing coming from inside a building. What on earth are they so happy about, singing like that? In frustration I kicked the door of the hall as I went past. I walked on to the corner of the passageway where I was due to meet Nick and Chris. There was no one there. I was very angry now, but perhaps it was the wrong corner. I walked back the way I'd come, and heard the singing again.

I opened the door and went inside. I sat down at the back of the hall, thinking how dreadful I felt, how hopeless and despairing. The singing stopped, and a man on the stage stood up and started to speak. I didn't know who he was and I couldn't follow what he was saying.

Then suddenly I heard him say, 'God can do anything, absolutely anything. I've seen him cure the drug addict, set the drug addict free, heal the sick, and I've witnessed him healing the mentally sick.' He seemed to be speaking directly to me, and I couldn't take it. I had to get out quickly.

I fled to the door, and a woman said to me, 'Would you like a cup of tea?' I refused. I wouldn't have been able to hold one anyway, I was shaking so much. She tried to persuade me.

'You're in a bit of a state, dear, but Jesus knows, he cares, he loves you.'

I really couldn't take any more. I went out and walked up the road, walking on and on, barefoot in the rain. Those words kept going round and round in my head, 'God can do anything, absolutely anything.' They rippled on the fringe of my despair. I didn't actually think about them, or what they might mean for me, but I became totally preoccupied with the words themselves.

I found myself walking back towards the hospital, those words pushing aside all other thoughts. I remember wondering at one point whether I could have talked to the speaker, but of course it was too late by then. I can't recall walking through the hospital grounds, but I do remember the stairs up to the ward, and feeling worried about how I would get in. I hesitated, for how long I have no idea, then a group of people came to the door, it was unlocked, and I went in with them.

The sister on duty commented calmly, 'Oh, you're back, are you?' and one of the other patients said, 'Did the police bring you back?' I must have said no, but what I most remember is being bewildered, probably at the lack of reaction. I felt lost, aware of noise around me, the clatter of plates, the movement of people; it all interrupted the words in my head.

I wasn't put into the locked room, despite the warning that I would be put back there if I ran away again, and the doctors seemed surprised at the improvement in me over the following days. My daily intake of prescribed drugs dropped sharply from thirty-plus tablets a day to eighteen, and I don't think that I ever thought of running away.

But in a way I'd only shifted from one preoccupation to another. Whereas I'd previously spent hours interpreting everything in the light of whatever thought had been uppermost in my mind — poison, or persecution, or relationships with a coffee mug or baked beans — now I related everything to what I'd heard about God. For instance, instead of being someone who carried a book everywhere with her, and who shouted at me about what was in it, Mollie now was someone who had a Bible which told her, and me, about God.

'God can do anything, absolutely anything.'

I told visitors what I'd heard. I listened to their conversations in the light of those words. People probably didn't talk of God or Christianity any more often than they'd done before, but to me it seemed now that I was surrounded by such ideas.

Some visitors to the ward one day told me that they knew of a group of people who would pray for me. Would I like that? I didn't know. Prayer implied to me a pilgrimage or a ceremony, but obviously they didn't mean that. And when they spoke of praying 'with me', I thought that it must mean some sort of personal contact, and that might be like fortune-telling or palmistry. I was frightened by the thought of palmistry, and that put me off.

On following visits, the suggestion was made again, but I was very indecisive. Could I cope, and what did I have to do? Why was it so difficult? Were they persecuting me? Did they want me to be frightened? Did they understand what was going on in my head? Did I have to make a decision? I couldn't face making the decision, but in the end I must have agreed.

I've no idea how they persuaded the hospital to let them take me out, because I was rarely allowed to leave Mead Park, and then only under strict supervision. But I know that I went to someone's house, and that there were several people present, drinking cups of tea in a room with a gas fire. It felt a bit like being in a consulting room with the doctors, but I was impressed that there was no psychiatric talk with its innuendoes and remarks, no attempts at group therapy, no pressure put on me to do what they wanted.

I felt very out of place. Inside me there was inexpressible turmoil and outside there was something which was new to me — a feeling of peace. But the two couldn't fit together. I couldn't sort out what they were saying. They were talking so calmly and quietly about Jesus and the power of God — a lot of words which I couldn't take in. They said that they were going to stand around me, and I wondered what they were going to do to me. Was that when they were going to start the questions and the group therapy?

They stood around me, and started talking again, but somehow not to each other. They were saying things about Jesus and the power of God, but why did they have to stand up to say it all over again? Were they talking to God? It was all very new and strange.

14

HEALING

People stood around me. They were praying for me. I was conscious of hands on my head, my back, my shoulders. I became aware of a sort of expectancy about what they would say next.

Then I heard and felt something shift in my head. Something within me was being moved towards an encounter with light. I was face to face with that light. I was being held within it. I knew it to be creative and positive, loving and peaceful, totally the opposite of the darkness I'd just left. I was completely enveloped by it, unaware of anything else, aware only of this wonderful presence.

The praying stopped.

I was stunned. I saw so clearly that I'd been ill, that for years I'd existed in a hell of mental illness, that I was now cured of that, suddenly, miraculously, in the space of a few moments. I couldn't put words to what had actually happened, but I knew, I understood. And the biggest thing was that there was hope now.

Someone asked me how I felt. They said that they believed God had done something in my life, and as I heard that, I realized clearly how very far from normal my life had been up to that point.

For the next few days I moved around in a peaceful haze, stunned, trying to adjust to my new awareness of life, my freedom from mental confusion and torment. I wasn't particularly joyful — I still had too many problems for that perhaps — but I had hope. The ripples which had spread across my despair, with those words 'God can do anything — absolutely anything', went very much deeper now. I saw them clearly and understood them — for I'd experienced the truth of them.

But something was still not right. I remembered those words, I remembered things I'd learned about Jesus as a child and I thought of the verses from the Bible which Mollie was always quoting. I lay in bed one night trying to work it out.

Suddenly I realized that even though I'd met God, that darkness had met light, and that I'd been drawn into that light and been healed, God was still on the outside. I had to ask Jesus to be in my life. I talked to him simply, telling him that I believed in him and wanted to follow him, so please would he come into my life and put right whatever was wrong. I told him how much I needed to know that he would be with me and guide me.

Then I became aware of his presence. The knowledge that he was willing to know me and to be with me — even though I was such a wreck, such a mess — overwhelmed me. I knew that he cared, that he understood what I'd been through and was giving my life a new direction. I wasn't alone any more. The pressure was gone. I could relate to God and I could communicate with him by praying.

15

BATTLING WITH ADDICTION

In the weeks that followed, life in Mead Park changed considerably for me. I was allowed a lot more freedom, such as bathing on my own, being allowed to choose whether or not I went to OT, and using a knife for my food. Previously I'd always had my food cut up for me, and in fact I was, I gather, considered to be the number one suspect if any piece of cutlery was missing — it was carefully counted after every meal!

I still had many problems, including the drug problem. And there were many emotional difficulties, as well as the horrific memories of all that had happened to me. All of these things would have to be sorted out. I was quite aware that through the continuous medication administered over several years I'd become addicted to various drugs, and while my tablet count now dropped still further from eighteen down to nine or twelve, it was going to be a great struggle to give this up completely — quite apart from the dependence I had on black-market drugs.

I was aware now of my surroundings, and therefore very conscious of the restrictions still imposed on me, conscious of the fact that I was no longer 'ill', and that, while I was still in a locked ward, the conditions which had necessitated the restrictions no longer existed. Time passed very slowly, but I did have the consolation of knowing that God was with me. The people who had prayed for me had given me a copy of Luke's Gospel, which I read, and sometimes I would get Mollie to read passages from her Bible. She would never part with it to let me read it myself, but she would often quote from it. With my awakened interest, I now listened and took notice.

It was my problem with drugs which made me run away again, abusing the privilege I now had of walking in the grounds with a nurse. I remember that we were sitting on a bench, and that there was a small garden shed a few yards away from us. I sauntered casually over to it and looked through the window to allay the nurse's suspicions. Then I suddenly disappeared round the side. At that she started to follow me, but I made a dash through the nearby bushes, and being able to run faster than her, I reached the gate and disappeared down a side road before she could catch me. I waited for a while, then made my way towards the centre of town.

At that point I intended to go to doctors' rooms and take prescriptions, but on the way I met a junkie friend and he gave me some drugs. I took them there and then. I felt very bad about all this, aware that I was moving backwards, for I was very conscious of my progress and my new commitment to Christianity. I knew that Christ had committed himself to me, and that I had to be active in my commitment to him. But my years in hospital had made me passive. Everything had been done for me for so long — nurses dressed me, bathed me, spoonfed me, made my bed, made every little decision for me. I was going to need a great deal of determination and purpose to follow this new path. Realizing that I'd so much to do almost defeated me before I began. I wondered whether I would ever be able to make it.

I knew that my continuing drug-taking was a separate problem, something quite apart from my previous mental state, and I felt very guilty about it. The fact was that the hospital had now cut down enormously on my tablets because of my changed state, and as a result I was no longer getting enough to deal with my addicted physical state. Both an ex-nurse and another ex-patient have confirmed in recent conversations that, at that time, over-prescribing was very common. I did find hard to accept without bitterness that it was originally the hospital treatment which addicted me to drugs. But at that time I was just angry at being in that predicament, and wondered, as I was to wonder many times, why God had healed my mind while not dealing with my desires for drugs. After all, how was I going to cope with that on top of all the memories and difficulties of my past? I was sure that God didn't approve of my drug-taking, but I just couldn't envisage ever being totally free of drugs.

I walked along the road and into a nearby graveyard with these thoughts going through my head. Since childhood I'd always been morbidly drawn towards graveyards, fascinated at the thought of the people who were buried there, and how they'd lived and died. I now realize that at this time I was 'coming down' from the effects of the drugs and my thoughts became increasingly morose.

I wondered whether I should go into the casualty department of a hospital and ask for help to get rid of the offending drugs in my system. I was aware that in giving up drugs this constant conflict, between not wanting to take anything, and physically needing something, was going to be a tremendous struggle. I knew that I was in a mess and talked myself into believing that I had to get out of it on my own.

Alone in that graveyard I wondered, 'Am I not being ungrateful for all that God has already done for me?' I never for a moment doubted my healing, but I did doubt whether I was really a Christian — if I was, surely it should have been easier than this?

I had no confidence in myself at all, and decided that I probably didn't have the will-power to master the situation. But on the other hand I suspected that I would get no help from the hospital. They seemed to deny all knowledge of my black-market drug-taking and so I was frightened to say anything. They might simply decide that I was mentally ill again and increase my hospital medication.

I stayed in the graveyard all night, then in the morning walked up the road, looking for a doctor's rooms. I'd decided not to try to steal prescriptions or drugs, but to go to see the doctor and if necessary explain my problem to him and seek his help. The receptionist at the surgery I went into was not too co-operative at first — not surprisingly, when I said that I wasn't a patient there. But eventually she showed me into the doctor's room. My first thought was that it reminded me of my mother's bedroom at home because everything was slightly askew — but perhaps it was because I wasn't seeing straight!

As I sat down my courage deserted me, and when he asked what he could do for me, I just said, 'I don't know.'

Without further preliminaries he asked, 'Have you been taking drugs for long?'

'Prescribed drugs,' I said curtly. I wasn't feeling at all well.

'Who is your doctor?'

'Er, I don't remember,' I mumbled.

'I think we should get someone else to have a look at you,' he suggested.

'I don't want to see any psychiatrists,' I told him.

'Why, have you seen them before?'

'Yes. In Mead Park. But I'm not going back there.'

'When were you in there?'

'A few days ago,' was all that I was prepared to admit to him.

'What was your problem?' was the next, inevitable, question.

I played it down. I wasn't going to tell him the whole story.

'I was depressed. But I'm not going back. They didn't help me.'

My voice must have betrayed my feelings, for he asked, 'Why are you so upset and angry with them?'

'I didn't like the way they treated me. Anyway, I'm better now. But they've given me so many tablets that I've got a drug problem now. That's what I want help with.'

'Well, you'll need hospital help with that problem, won't you? I'll have to see what I can arrange.'

'I don't want to go to hospital again. Hospitals won't help me. They'll just give me more tablets. They don't understand,' I sobbed at him.

Then I vomited.

He was trying to help, but I got so cross with him. 'Are you blind?' I shouted. 'I've got a drug problem. Can't you help me? I can't do it on my own.'

He took me upstairs, and told me to wait while he did some telephoning, saying that I could lie down if I wanted to. The receptionist kept popping in and out to check up on me. I've no idea how long I was there, but eventually I was taken downstairs again.

The doctor said, 'I rang Mead Park.'

My heart sank. What on earth had they said about me?

'I suggested that we send you to Brooklands,' he continued. 'And they've agreed.'

I started to protest that I didn't want to go back to a hospital, but he cut me short.

'You must understand that you're still 'on section', and that will have to continue. You're not free to go where you want, you know. We'll get you to Brooklands now. Mr Lee from Mead Park will be there to see you when you arrive.'

When we got to the hospital, I was taken into an office where Mr Lee was waiting with a Brooklands doctor and a nurse. Mr Lee started by giving me a lecture on messing about with drugs. 'How long have you been taking black-market drugs?' he asked.

I didn't answer him directly, but said, 'I hate drugs. It's wrong to take them. I'm a Christian now, and I know that it's wrong. Why on earth did you give me so many tablets when I was ill? That's how it all started.'

I was still feeling very nauseous, and they just left me hunched up on a chair in the corner of the room while they debated what to do with me. They talked about me, but not to me. If only they'd said that they understood the problem and would help me, it would have been easier, but they didn't even convey to me that they recognized my present difficulty or that they had any idea of the dilemma I was in. It seemed to me at the time that they were going more on my past condition than on the present one. I think that I was beginning to become institutionalized, just part of the furniture, someone to be dealt with from accumulated notes! To be fair, my notes must have shown that I hadn't been an easy patient, and even though I knew that I'd been healed, they must have been puzzled and wondered whether it would be permanent.

Then the Brooklands doctor turned to me and said, 'We'll have you here, Liesl, but only on the understanding that there will be no drugs on the premises. We'll put you in the group therapy clinic, where you were before.'

My recollections of group therapy had been rather hazy, but that was of course due to my mental state when I'd been there before. Now I was very aware of my surroundings. The large functional rooms, furnished with drab and dilapidated chairs and tables, the dirty paintwork, the creaking floorboards upstairs, the long noisy corridors, all this scarcely encouraged anyone to a positive and forward-looking attitude. Everywhere was a frustrating air of emptiness and aimlessness.

I feel sure that if I'd been kept occupied, less bored, it would not have been so difficult. Going back there recently just to look around, it seemed that nothing had changed — not even the torn wallpaper. I was particularly struck by the total absence of any books or magazines, any indication of any activity, social or otherwise. There wasn't even a television set, as far as I could see.

16

MURDER

There was a commotion in the hall outside, and someone shouted, 'Get out of the way, Liesl.'

Then Steve, one of the group, came into the room. He was very angry, and was hiding something in his sleeve. I had no idea I was in danger. But as he stretched out his arm, I saw the carving knife. I jumped up onto the window sill, and he lunged at me, stabbing me in the ribs. Someone tackled him, knocking him out. I realized that Steve's intention had been to murder me.

For what seemed like the first time since I'd been in hospital, everyone was most sympathetic and concerned. Steve was taken off to another part of the hospital and I didn't see him again. The incident shook me, for I was very aware once again that I'd been close to death.

The group therapy sessions at Brooklands were described by one friend who visited me as 'open chaos'.

'Everything was happening at once,' she said. 'There was one big buzz of talk. It was bizarre enough to drive one mad!'

I still had a great aversion to getting involved with the sessions, but I had felt sorry for Steve. He was deaf and dumb. So, using the deaf and dumb language learned from my mother, I'd sometimes interpreted for him. I knew that this was being used as a means of drawing me into the sessions, and I didn't like it. On that day I'd refused to help, and left. It was as I walked into the day-room that he attacked me.

On another occasion Joan was very upset, and started crying and shouting abuse at everyone. She stormed out, but no one followed or took any notice. I got up to go.

'Where are you going, Liesl?' I was asked. 'Do you feel the need to get up to be noticed?'

'I don't think you should be noticing me,' I replied. 'You should be getting on with your job.'

I found Joan in the day-room, still crying. I sat down next to her.

'They don't care a damn, do they?' she sobbed.

'I care,' I tried to assure her. 'What's the matter?'

She told me her story, then opened her bag to show me her store of Driminal.

'They don't care if I take a hundred of these. But I came here to stop taking them,' she said.

'Those won't help you. Why don't you throw them out?'

She became abusive. 'Look at you. You're a fine one to talk! You take drugs.'

'Well, what are you going to do about it?' I asked her.

'Kill myself.'

'That's not an answer to your problem, and I know that drugs are not an answer to problems,' I told her. 'I found that God was the answer to a problem that I had.'

'I can't understand you having a drug problem now,' she said. 'But you're young. There's no hope for me.'

'I used to think that there was no hope for me,' I replied.

My life definitely had a new sense of direction, a

purpose to it, but it became a constant battle. I couldn't ever quite manage to get the hurdle of the drugs out of the way. I'd succeed for a few days, then slip again. I knew that I had to break this pattern, but emotionally it was very difficult. I'd become depressed, and then get concerned because depression had been such a familiar part of my illness.

It would have helped a great deal if I could have talked to another Christian, especially about my healing and conversion, but those were still very private experiences and I was afraid of becoming a spectacle again if I talked about them. I certainly didn't want it all to be analyzed at a group therapy session — it was much too precious to be torn apart like that! In any case, people there never seemed to talk about things in a normal conversational way. I suppose that I'd been in the habit for so long of not communicating, that I just didn't have a great urge to start sharing my thoughts.

I considered going to talk to the hospital chaplain, as it seemed he should be able to help and advise me. I thought of asking him to pray with me about my drug problem, and my other emotional problems. But then I started to wonder why he didn't pray with the other people in group therapy. I came to the conclusion that I'd little confidence in him.

He was a man of about forty-five, of stocky build, with a too-clean dog-collar which somehow always made me feel that there should be a lead attached to it. He seemed to live in just one grey suit, and his head appeared to bob in time with his words, as if there was a clockwork mechanism inside him! His speech had a very monotonous quality to it, an evenness of tone and pace, no doubt in his mind exuding calmness and tranquillity to disturbed patients! He always answered a question with another question. In fact, every statement he made was in the form of a question. I decided that he wouldn't understand my conversion experience, but would probably just say, with his head bobbing, 'You feel the need to tell me that?'

At times I felt angry with God for having sorted out my mental problem instead of the drug problem. Why couldn't he have done it the other way round? I certainly didn't doubt his ability to deal with the matter, although I don't think I actually prayed specifically about it at that stage. It was a very difficult time, and I just prayed that I might find a way out of the muddle that I was in.

My life seemed to consist of an endless spiral of taking drugs, not taking drugs, the bad times, the guilt, and a lack of confidence in my own ability to walk God's way. I worried too that I might accidentally take an overdose and die. I knew now that my life was not mine to throw away, and so I had no intention of committing suicide, but it could have happened unintentionally.

It was all so frustrating. I was disappointed and impatient with God and myself. He'd helped me before, so why didn't he do it again? And yet I felt that I was being ungrateful. The trouble was that I had nobody there to explain to me that God works in many different ways.

17

JUNKIE PARTY

Brooklands had laid down the condition of 'no drugs on the premises'. This bothered me. I interpreted it to mean that I shouldn't be in possession of drugs, rather than not taking them. I was there to get free from the problem, but no one seemed to care what happened, and that made it harder to care myself.

The general lack of supervision on the ward made it all too easy to exchange drugs right there. In fact, it was easier and safer than doing so in the centre of town where one had to be on the watch for the police. But I did know that several people had been thrown out of the unit for having drugs, and I was frightened that the same might happen to me. I realized that if it did, I wouldn't be able to cope on my own at that stage. I really did want to co-operate, but just didn't seem to be able to discipline my will, and I didn't know who to turn to for help. It seemed as if the staff had almost lost their understanding of 'normality'. If someone made a fuss and acted 'disturbed' he or she received attention, but a normal request for help, a simply-stated plea that one was finding it difficult to cope, gained scant sympathy.

I did have quite a lot of freedom at that time. We were allowed out in the afternoons from two until four, and sometimes in the mornings between the group therapy session and lunch. On those days I would often go into the little chapel in the grounds of the hospital. I preferred being there on my own to taking part in the Sunday services.

It was quite against the rules to go out in the evenings, but I did this from time to time. On one such outing I set off with Bob, from the other ward, in a borrowed car to get to a party outside the town. We planned to pick up some friends on the way, but when we arrived at their home to collect them, they were having a flaming row. There was shouting, and the door burst open. The wife stormed out, followed by the husband.

'What's going on here?' I asked Bob.

'Don't ask me,' he said. 'Let's go!'

'I'm not going anywhere. I feed bad. You go on, and get me something.'

'No, you come with me. You're more likely to get junk than I am,' argued Bob.

'Just roll me some fags, then go,' I insisted.

Eventually he agreed and left. He came back later with some drugs which I had all at once. Then I made my way back to the hospital. When I got there, they put me in a side ward, gave me a good talking to and left me. I was very upset. I knew I'd let God down again. I wondered why he'd helped me if I was going to continue like this. Maybe I wasn't trying hard enough to fight the drug problem. Perhaps I gave in too easily. I felt that I was swimming against the tide, and where was the hope of winning?

Not long after that I went to another drug party. This one I remember very vividly. I'd been told that it would be in Greg's room on the second floor of a house in the centre of town. There would be a name on the door, but I was not to walk straight in. The instructions were to ring three times, wait, ring three more times, wait again, and then I'd be let in.

I made my way to the house in a state of some excitement and anticipation. I went along a small alleyway, through a black gate and across a tiny yard littered with broken crockery and old tins, jam jars and other debris — a squalid place. I rang the bell as I'd been told but nobody came to the door, so I went in and up the stairs. The hallway was dark and damp, and there was a feeling of emptiness throughout the house, as though no one lived there. I found the door with the name Greg on it, and knocked. I got no answer so I went in.

The room was full of smoke. There were about a dozen people there, lounging around, all obviously drugged out of their minds. A thin, pale man with patched jeans and no T-shirt was half lying across an old chair, his bruised, needle-marked arms hanging limply. Someone else was standing in the middle of the room talking to, and answering, himself in an agitated fashion. I saw a girl with a syringe, but she couldn't manage to use it, and she started crying out for help in an aggressive way. But no one bothered with her.

Someone stumbled across the room to the sink area, presumably to get himself a drink.

'Have you brought David with you?' he asked me.

'Which David?' I replied.

Then the man in the middle of the room started chanting, 'I think he's fluffed it. I think David's fluffed it.' Then with a stream of obscenities he complained that David could at least have brought them some stuff before he died.

The man at the sink said, 'David should have been dead years ago.'

I looked around the room. The whole scene struck me in a new light — it was so totally selfish, uncaring, repulsive. There was a young chap in a corner leaning against the wall. He looked as if he might have been dead, but they weren't concerned about him, any more than they'd been concerned about David. They were just out for what they could get, with no compassion or humanity left for others.

I stood there, upset and rather frightened now. Then I noticed a naked couple in a far corner of the room. That was the last straw. The crude, degrading attitude to sex was one aspect of the drug scene that I'd never been able to take. I was suddenly and clearly aware of how sordid and corrupt it all was.

I turned my back on it and left.

18

FRIENDS

After that party I made a conscious decision not to take any more hospital pills. I felt that by taking them I was feeding my problem. So I accepted the tablets which were handed out every four hours, but I didn't swallow them, hiding them under my tongue instead and then flushing them down the loo. I knew that I could have given them to the other patients, but then I would have been feeding their problems for them. The deception and the waste of money when I threw them away made me feel guilty, but I was afraid of refusing them because in the past that had meant an injection. Also, I suppose that I still lacked confidence in my ability to manage without them. This way I had the security of knowing that the next dose would be there if I really needed it.

At first it was very hard, and there were times when I did swallow my tablets. There were other times when I had little choice in the matter, for the nurse on duty would decide to check under my tongue before I had a chance to dispose of them. But such occasions became fewer and fewer. There were some days when I did come perilously close to giving up, to deciding that it was all too much for me. But I prayed that God would help me in this struggle, and he showed me that he doesn't always come through the clouds with an instant miracle. Sometimes his answers come in different forms.

There were often visitors at group therapy

sessions. Sometimes people came in to observe us, as if we were specimens to be looked at. Perhaps because I was younger than most of the patients, I attracted more than my share of attention. I disliked this intensely, for I needed normal friendship, not this abnormal interest.

At this time, some theological students were doing a six-week course at the hospital as part of their training. I don't think I particularly noticed them, but one day when I was out I met some of them in a cafe. One of them said, 'Hello, Liesl,' and beckoned me over. I realized where I'd seen him before. He was Roger Butler, one of the students, and as I sat down with him and his friend — and helped them eat their chips! — we started talking about Brooklands. I told them how much I wanted to get out of there. I felt that I could trust Roger in a way that I couldn't trust the doctors, for since he was training for the ministry his advice would be in line with what God wanted.

'Can you find out for me about the "on Section" bit?' I asked him. 'And also how I can get around it. It looks as if it will only be cancelled when I've proved that I can manage outside the hospital system. And how can I provide that proof while I'm confined within the system? It's a vicious circle.' And I knew that all the hospital records would tell against me.

'I'll see what I can find out,' Roger promised. Then he invited me to visit his home to meet his wife. I said that I had to get back to Brooklands, but would very much like to visit them another time.

The next day Margaret, Roger's wife, came to the hospital. She said that it would be easier for me to visit them if I'd already met her. We chatted for a bit, and she invited me to go to supper with them, and made all the necessary arrangements with the hospital staff.

I was very nervous about the visit. Roger picked me up and drove me to their home, which seemed to be miles away through open country. It felt very strange going out like that, and I was rather apprehensive. Would I cope socially? Would I be able to eat their food? Would they mind my patched jeans and bare feet? Would I be able to ask to leave if I wanted to?

But as Roger opened the door of their little cottage, the cosiness and friendliness of it struck me, and immediately I felt more at ease. It was so different from anything I was used to. Brought up in a large house, trained in a big hospital, and then confined for so long in the emptiness and clinical atmosphere of Mead Park and Brooklands, it was so different from anything I had known.

I exclaimed as I went into the tiny living room, 'Oh, isn't this quaint? It's like a doll's house!'

'Yes, we like it here,' agreed Roger.

'It's just as well you're not six-foot-four! You'd keep banging your head.'

'I'd have to go around on my knees,' joked Roger. 'Would you like a glass of sherry?'

I refused. I wasn't sure whether I should drink alcohol.

Margaret, who'd been in the kitchen when we arrived, came in and said hello and put a record on. It was jazz.

'Do you like jazz?' Roger asked me.

'Yes I do,' I said. I noticed a violin in the corner of the room. 'Who plays the violin?'

'Oh, that's Margaret's. Do you play any instrument?'

I explained that I'd learned the piano as a child, but had always wanted to play the drums. 'But I'm really not very musical,' I added.

Then we had supper. It was all very relaxed and comfortable. I suddenly realized that I was talking quite freely to them, communicating normally with normal people for the first time in years. They asked me about myself, showing a genuine interest and concern.

'How long have you been in Brooklands, Liesl?'

'Too long' was my simple answer. 'I really do want to get out. I don't think being there is doing me any good.'

'Why do you say that?' Margaret asked.

'Well, I'm there because I've messed about with drugs. And there are drugs on the ward so it's hard to get away from it. And nobody seems to care what you do.' I turned to Roger. 'What do you think of the place?'

'I find it interesting. I'm very glad to have the opportunity to be there,' he replied. 'But how on earth did you get involved in drug-taking in the first place?'

I still found it difficult to talk about my stay in Mead Park without being very emotional, so I said briefly that I'd been there after a breakdown, and that I'd been given a lot of drugs there which had addicted me.

'I'd never have gone into the drug scene otherwise,' I told them. 'I'm clear of the habit now, but I'm still finding it difficult, and I'm still on prescribed drugs.'

'I've noticed that you sometimes seem very depressed at the group therapy sessions, Liesl,' Roger said. He painted a black picture of me, but I assured them that I was very much better than I had been. I explained again that I felt that I'd reached the stage where Brooklands wasn't helping me.

'I think I'm becoming institutionalized. Since I became a Christian, my life has had a new direction to it because of my commitment, but I just have no confidence in my ability to go out into the world and get a job and cope with ordinary life. I've been away from it all for so long.'

I washed up for them after supper, amused by Margaret's romantic little kitchen. I wondered whether it was up to me to ask to be taken back or whether Roger would suggest it. In the event he announced that the hospital had made the condition I be back there by ten. It had been a real treat to be in a 'normal' home.

The Butlers both visited me frequently after that evening. Roger came almost every day for a while, and Margaret hardly less often. I used to ask Roger a lot of questions, like 'Why are you going to be a clergyman?' and 'What do you really think about drugs and drug-taking?' and 'Do you believe that God can heal people?' Roger patiently answered my questions one by one. He explained that he'd been an organ scholar at Cambridge, and talked about his student life there. I enjoyed hearing about that, as it seemed to help me fill in some of the missing years of my life. He said that he'd felt called to the Christian ministry. I was very conscious that because of his calling I trusted him, and would listen to him and accept his advice. I suppose I was aware at that time that I needed leading, for I had no involvement with any church.

I could not see how the church style I'd been brought up with — of hats and twin-sets, hand-shaking and polite conversation — could ever fit in with my personal Christianity. I imagined that the formal church-goers would probably feel contaminated if they had to associate with someone who'd had my problems. At the same time I recognized a need for structure in my Christian life. I've always been grateful for this legacy from my upbringing in the Catholic church. At that time I had the feeling that I was facing it alone with God. It was only some years later that I came to understand that we should all be facing things together as God's people, fellow-Christians.

When I talked to Roger, I sometimes wondered whether he questioned my commitment because I was still in Brooklands. I often considered whether to tell him about my healing. His answer to my tentative question on that general subject had been that, while he was quite sure that God could and did heal, he personally had never been involved in any such experience. So I didn't tell him, because I wasn't sure that I could make him understand what it had been like in Mead Park, and the horror of it all. I feared that if he didn't understand it, the healing would have no significance for him.

These visits were a great help to me, for we would have long discussions about God. They were discussions of the sort that most people have before they're converted.

Is Jesus really alive? Is it important for people to go to church? Why is there suffering in the world?

I think I was trying to discover how I could have reached the answers before I'd sorted out the arguments. It was a question of involving my head in the faith which was already in my heart.

In the course of these discussions Roger told me what he'd found out about the 'section' situation. I was still being held 'on Section', he said. I found that rather depressing if not unexpected. But one evening he came into the hospital with another student and told me that he'd been discussing me with Margaret.

'We'd really like to help you if we can,' he said. 'We've decided that, if the hospital will agree, we'll take you to live with us for a while, and help you to find a job. How do you feel about that idea?'

I was very excited at the prospect, and at the same time aware that this would be a great challenge. I was not at all confident of my ability to cope with life, or do any sort of job. I also felt that in all fairness I should tell them more about myself, especially that I'd attempted suicide. Again I wondered about telling them of my healing.

I was extremely disappointed to find that Brooklands rejected any idea of my staying with the Butlers. So now getting out became even more important to me. I asked Paul, a patient who knew a little about the law, whether he had any knowledge of the 'Section' regulation under which I was being held. He told me that he had an idea that if I could stay out of hospital for twenty-eight days, without being caught or being a nuisance to the public or the police, the section would automatically expire.

When Roger came to visit me again, I told him what Paul had said about the twenty-eight-day rule.

'If that's true, will you let me come and stay with you? I really can't take being in hospital any longer, and I'm not sure that I'd be able to cope with the outside world on my own, especially for those first twenty-eight days.'

I told him that I was now clear of the drug problem but not clear of drugs altogether. I had recurring pain in my arms and so had been put back onto barbiturates and chloral hydrate at night to help me sleep and DF118s during the day. I'd been addicted to all of those from Mead Park days. This upset me and my mind was full of conflict over it. I needed the medication for the pain, but I was afraid that taking it might start the whole cycle of addiction off again.

I knew that so long as I had to take any tablets at all, the problem wasn't totally over. I so much wanted to be able to say, once and for all, to Roger and to everyone else, 'I do not take drugs.'

19

A NEW PERSPECTIVE

The prospect of getting out of Brooklands and staying with Roger and Margaret excited me. If only I could be free of the 'Section', and given a chance. But Roger only said that he'd have to ask the hospital. I pleaded with him not to. They'd said no before, and I was terrified that they'd do so again.

'If I go off the rails or do anything silly, just put me in the car and bring me back here,' I said. 'But please give me the chance to prove that I'm OK'.

He left saying that he'd think about it.

The next day I went to see Margaret during her lunch hour, explaining again how I felt about getting out of the hospital, and how I needed support to prove to others, and to myself, that I could cope with a normal life. She and Roger must have talked it over, for that evening he came to the hospital to say that they'd have me. So the next day I simply left the hospital and made my way to their home. That tiny cottage was so different from Brooklands — so warm, so friendly.

I hoped Roger and Margaret knew what they were taking on, and wondered whether they'd be able to tolerate me. And I was bothered about whether what we were doing could be regarded as law-breaking, for I realized that as Christians we had a duty to uphold the law. I decided that the section regulation was designed for the protection of others, and that as I wasn't going to harm anyone or break the law in any way, it was all right.

It was bewildering to be out of hospital and living in a normal home. So many little things were different, and I kept worrying that Roger and Margaret would misinterpret my reactions. I was very aware that they'd accepted the responsibility for me. In retrospect, I think they must have had some agreement with the hospital, for my friendship with them was known, and the authorities would have surely checked with them if they were searching for me. If that was the case, they wisely didn't tell me, and so held me to the need to prove myself.

I was aware too that Roger and Margaret had not been married for very long, and feared that I was an intruder. Then I realized that I didn't actually know Margaret very well, and wasn't sure what she wanted me to do, or not to do, in the house.

It was all so different from being locked up in a hospital situation. Any restrictions on me were now those of social convention, friendship and good manners rather than imposed rules. It was wonderful to be able to have a bath when I wanted without comment or explanation; to make myself a cup of coffee when I wanted one, rather than have to wait for the set time or go out to the cafe in the grounds and buy one; to read a book for the sheer pleasure of reading, without being accused of 'hiding behind a book'.

Meal times, too, were a social occasion — such a contrast. My experience had been of a large group of fifty or more sitting at utilitarian tables with very basic crockery and cutlery and institution food. There had been no conversation and no real interest in whether anyone ate or not.

I enjoyed the home cooking and the day-to-day conversation which was not an attempt at psychiatric counselling.

Even the practical aspects were different. I found that I was nervous if I had to set the table, for it was so long since that sort of thing had mattered. When I washed up for Margaret, she always thanked me. In Brooklands I'd have been accused of seeking attention by doing any such chores; every action had to be given a psychiatric explanation.

Contact with other people, too, was on a very different basis. Visitors to the Butlers' home were normal, friendly, interested in each other and in me, whereas visitors or new admissions at Brooklands had tended to be noisy and self-centred. I was constantly struck by the variety of clothes which people had, and how they seemed to wear something different every day. I think I tended to be rather introspective, not very outgoing, and visitors' questions often threw me off balance. What could I say to things like 'Where did you live before you came here?' and 'What is your job?'

When I went out I felt conspicuous. It was strange walking past people and being free to stop and talk, and for the most part not even having to worry about whether they would report me to the authorities. Of course, I was very nervous about being caught, and that made me rather insecure. I wondered whether I would be sent back to Mead Park if I was found. Or if for some reason I did ever need to go back there, would I be able to, or would they refuse to have me? I counted off the days, feeling uncomfortably sure that I'd be caught before the time was up.

One day I met Margaret in town during her

lunch hour. Afterwards I was walking past a small stationer's shop when I noticed a card in the window advertising for a temporary assistant. I reasoned that if I had a job, I'd be able to use that as an argument for being allowed to stay out of hospital, proof that I was really able to cope. So I went in, somewhat nervously, wondering what questions I'd be asked about my past, my previous experience, and so on. But the manager just agreed to take me on, starting the next day. I was delighted — even the idea of being able to go to work felt really good, and as I walked on my way I thanked God that someone had wanted to employ me.

It was a small shop, rather cramped and stuffy, and I found work very exhausting at first, especially on the arms and feet. Somehow, my customers were always the ones wanting things from the top shelves. I was rather clumsy, and not very good at adding up. Nonetheless the manager must have found me amusing rather than annoying, for he agreed to keep me on for a second week, even though it was obvious that the job and I were not ideally suited!

I remember my first lunch break and my sense of freedom and achievement at being a normal working girl again. And when one day I was asked to be responsible for opening up the shop the following morning, I was thrilled. I was aware of my ignorance about the job and everything that went with it, but still very diffident about asking too many questions in case they got cross with me. In hospital I'd got used to people's annoyance as the response to making enquiries. The variety of people who came into the shop was endlessly fascinating to me. I was intrigued by their clothes, and by the make-up the women wore. Did they put all that on every day?

At first I used to go into a nearby church for part of my lunch hour, but somehow I didn't feel at home. I had a fear that the vicar would come in, wonder what I was doing and suspect that there was something wrong with me. And if he did speak to me, and ask me my name and where I lived, it would be awkward to answer. It was a relief when I realized that God was with me in the street and in coffee bars as well as in churches, and so I decided to spend the time out of doors or in a cafe instead.

On one occasion I bumped into some old nursing friends, and we had coffee together. Naturally they asked what I'd been doing. They were under the impression that I'd only been in Mead Park for a few weeks and had then moved away to another part of the country. I didn't disillusion them. But then they asked me about my close friends, Joan and Gwen, thinking that I'd have news of them. They must have thought little of me for being so non-committal, but of course I really could not answer their questions.

I turned the conversation to talk about more general things. I found it interesting to catch up on their news and for the first time I realized fully what I'd missed through being in hospital for so long. Perhaps that was the first time I was truly aware of having missed my nursing finals.

At work I found I had difficulty in reading the labels on the boxes high up on the shelves, so I went to have my eyes tested. That struck me as an essentially normal thing to do. I suppose I remember this because I was constantly asking myself whether I was doing the 'normal' thing, and whether those around me saw me as 'normal'. And it was such a pleasure to have money to use in the way I wanted — sensible, constructive ways, such as buying toothpaste and Mars Bars! And of course I gave some to Margaret for my keep.

When the twenty-eight days were up at last I went back to Brooklands, confident that I could now come and go as I pleased.

Roger had suggested that I continue as a day patient for a while. This would give me something to do until I found another job, and having to get there and back every day was helpful discipline for me. There wasn't very much to keep me occupied at home when both Roger and Margaret were out all day. Also, the feeling of familiarity with everything at the hospital gave me a sense of security, as I hadn't yet become fully assimilated to normal living.

Above all, to me it was an act of defiance to walk in and out at will. I had to show that I was all right, and I wanted them to acknowledge that I was all right, too.

That first time, I simply arrived and walked into group therapy, said hello and sat down. There was a complete lack of reaction, which disappointed me. I'd thought that at least some of them would be pleased to see me, or even simply curious, and I was rather deflated! The session seemed to be even more chaotic and noisy than I remembered, with the endless questions, and games, and people constantly on the move. I'd made far more progress than I'd realized, and I was relieved to know that I could now walk out whenever I wanted to. I was pleased too that I now had the opportunity to show others that it was possible to get out and to make a go of things.

After the session I met the consultant in the

corridor, and he asked me where I'd been.

'I've been living with friends, and I've had a job,' I informed him.

'How are you?' he enquired.

'OK.'

'I suppose that in your absence you've been drugged out of your little mind,' he commented sarcastically. I was very offended by his remark. Then he went on, 'Well, Liesl, you can give it a try. But I expect we'll see you back here.'

I asked him, 'Do you think that I'm better than when I first came here?'

'Well, I suppose I must admit that you are, yes.'

'I'm certainly much better than when I was in Mead Park.'

'I gather so.'

'Aren't you interested in why I'm better?' I asked him.

'You tell me.'

'I believe in God, you see. I have more confidence in him healing than I have in you lot. He knows what goes on inside, but you can only deal with what you see from the outside.'

He said nothing, just turned and walked on down the corridor.

20

PUTTING RIGHT THE PAST

Those days with Margaret and Roger at the cottage gave me an increasing security and independence as I looked for another job and attended group therapy sessions. But as I made the daily adjustments to 'normal' living, I realized that there were some things from my past which had to be put right.

One morning I left the cottage on my scooter to go to Brooklands. A few hundred yards down the road I turned back to collect my crash helmet, not for safety's sake — wearing a helmet was not compulsory in those days — but simply to keep my ears warm on a rather cold morning! Thank goodness I did! As I went around a busy roundabout, my brakes failed. The next thing I knew I was in an ambulance on my way to hospital. I was concussed, had a dislocated jaw and needed a few stitches. After a couple of days in hospital I was allowed to go home again, but my scooter was a write-off. I remembered that the day before the spare wheel and speedometer cable had been missing when I left Brooklands. Roger had suggested I inform the police, but I hadn't bothered. Now the police suspected that the brakes had been tampered with, but they never found out who did it.

While I was lying in the hospital I saw Nurse Sims standing talking to someone at the desk. She was the nurse who had coped with me after my

Carbutal overdose. I'd screamed at her and been very uncooperative, for in my confused mental state I'd been convinced that the drips were an invasion into me, and had repeatedly tried to pull them out of my veins. Now I asked where she was working, and the next day when I was allowed out of bed went up to find her ward, glad of the opportunity to apologize for my behaviour in the past.

She obviously recognized me at once. She said 'Oh, are you back in here? Another overdose?'

'No, a scooter crash,' I explained. It was difficult to speak because of my dislocated jaw. 'Overdose days are over. I have a new way of life now, and there are a lot of things to put straight from my past. I felt God wanted me to come up and apologize to you for my behaviour. I really am sorry.'

She thanked me for my apology. 'You were very disturbed then, but it's nice to see you better now.'

I also felt very guilty about the times I'd stolen prescriptions from doctors' rooms, and drugs from pharmacists. Gradually over the following months I visited the places I could remember, explaining what I'd done and apologizing. Needless to say, it was always very difficult, and I was terrified that someone would decide to prosecute me. But no one ever did.

I'd walk up and down outside a chemist's shop, trying to pluck up courage to go in, waiting until the shop was empty, and at the same time trying to talk myself into believing that it wasn't really necessary to go in and explain. But I knew it was something that God wanted me to do, and eventually I'd go inside.

The reactions I got were varied. On the whole

113

they were unemotional, almost disinterested at times. Some gave me little lectures. For instance, I'd start off by saying to the assistant something like, 'I'm not sure whether I should speak to you or to the pharmacist. It's about something I did here which I'm very sorry about. I stole a prescription for some sleeping draught. I think it was made out to a Mrs Lowe. I presented it to you here.'

'Oh, when was this?'

'A while ago. I pretended that I was Mrs Lowe, and collected it.'

Looking somewhat uncertain about what to do or say, the assistant called the pharmacist. I repeated my story, adding, 'I'm very sorry. I know it was wrong and foolish.'

'Yes, it was,' agreed the pharmacist, as dumbfounded and nonplussed as his assistant.

'Well, it won't happen again,' I assured him, and left, glad to be out of the shop. I was sorry that he hadn't asked me what had happened to change me, and wished I'd had the courage to volunteer the information that God had helped me and changed my life. But it was such a long story, I felt daunted at the prospect of going through it all, stage by stage, to try and make people understand.

21

INDEPENDENCE

Now I was ready to make the next big step forwards. There were a few disappointments in my job-hunting but eventually I found a job as a dental receptionist. At first sight it seemed ideal for me in view of my nursing training. As I was still finding my feet I thought it would be a good idea to have a job which I could cope with quite easily. But in the event it put an awful lot of pressure on me, partly because of the ever-present availability of drugs, which was something I had not bargained for, and partly because one of the partners was an alcoholic, a condition I always found difficult to cope with, on account of my mother's problem.

Having a job meant that I could move out of the Butlers' home and into a flat. I shared with two other girls, Liz, who was a student, and Elaine, who worked in a language department of the university. Roger and Margaret saw the move as a sign of my progress, but I was still very much under their wing, visiting them a great deal and often spending a night or two back with them. I knew that they would be moving before long, as Roger was finishing his training and I was very concerned about what I'd do without them. I valued their care and support enormously, for without them everything would have been so much more difficult. I really did see them as God's answer to my prayer for help in my struggle against drugs and depression. They were so patient and tolerant, and made me feel like a real person again.

The flat I moved into was the upper floor of a small semi, with a large bedroom in the loft which I shared with Liz.

I loved the freedom of coming and going as I pleased. Even though we all led our own separate lives, we were friendly to each others' visitors, and there always seemed to be a lot going on. Martin, who had visited me in Mead Park, called occasionally and so did the Butlers, of course, as well as various other students I'd met through them. I remember that my sister came several times to see me, and I was very proud to be able to show the flat off to her, and to introduce her to my friends. I'd come a long way from Mead Park and Brooklands days.

I went out a lot to parties, or spent evenings with friends. On such occasions the subject of palmistry seemed to keep cropping up, as it had often done at Brooklands. People generally are fascinated by fortune-telling and horoscopes, although most would insist that they don't take it seriously. I knew, from my nursing days, that there was a power involved, but hadn't then recognized it as the power of Satan.

In Brooklands my palm-reading had been very casual, and I hadn't consciously seen it as evil, but now I began to see it in a different light. Yet I still had the feeling that I wanted to read hands. I knew that I could do it and would enjoy doing it, even though I was aware it was wrong. I wondered why I felt so attracted to the idea. Even then it didn't occur to me that my involvement with palmistry was something which I should turn away from as a definite choice.

I remember one party in particular. It was a rather awkward group and hard to keep the conversation going. The topic of fortune-telling came up. One of the guests said in a joking sort of way, 'I've never had my palm read. I've always wanted to.'

His girlfriend replied, 'Oh, it's all rubbish. I had it done once, and nothing came true.'

I was challenged by that. I knew that palm-reading was wrong, but in order to prove that it was evil I had to demonstrate that it could work. So I took hold of her hand and studied her palm. Then looking at them both I asked her, 'Have you told Richard about your abortion?'

She became very upset and flustered. Someone asked her if it was true, but she wouldn't answer, just got up and left the room in tears. Then, of course, everyone else wanted me to read their hands, but I said no, explaining that it was wrong.

And I never did it again.

Having a normal social life again was fun. I felt secure and relaxed enough to allow my own natural eccentricity to show! For instance, I remember planting daffodil bulbs at one o'clock in the morning much to the amusement of a passing policeman. And another time a college friend called in with his girlfriend on their way to a party. She bemoaned the fact that she'd always wanted straight hair, so I told her that my sister had said hair could be straightened if it was ironed under brown paper. Out came the ironing board and an old brown paper bag! It worked, though not for long!

But there was another side of the coin. The town had too many memories for me, and I came to realize that as long as I stayed there I wouldn't get away from what had happened. This was brought home to me one lunch hour when I bumped into someone I'd known as a 'pusher'.

He asked me if I'd seen Alex, and when I replied, 'No, I'm not in the scene now,' he just sniggered scornfully.

'It sounds as if you don't believe me,' I said. I wanted very much to convince him. 'Surely the fact that I've put on weight proves that I'm off drugs.' He said nothing, and walked away.

Then I turned back and told him what I thought of him pushing drugs — he didn't take them himself. 'You're only interested in money, you don't care about people, you're evil!'

He just stared at me blankly, completely without emotion, and didn't reply at all. Of course, my outburst didn't put anything right, but it did help my feelings a bit. And it left me wondering how I could reach such people.

I'd thought rather naively that if I could tell them about Jesus, that would be all that was needed. But I came to realize that they didn't listen or understand. Their lives were so bound up with deceit and lies and mistrust that they couldn't trust what I said about Jesus Christ. The only way to reach them would be to spend time with them and show them the truth through my own lifestyle. But at that time I was aware that I needed to get away from the whole scene and make a completely fresh start to my life. It was very frustrating.

I wanted people to know what had happened to me, but it wasn't easy to talk about it all. I had to be sure that it would be taken seriously.

I soon learned that almost invariably one of the first questions people ask when you talk about Christianity or a miraculous experience is, 'What

118

church do you belong to?' Having to admit that I didn't actually belong to any church at that time didn't help.

Looking back, I feel that it was a pity that I didn't or couldn't join a church fellowship immediately after my conversion. At the time I had no idea of the meaning and strength of a body of Christians who are able to help and encourage each other. Going off to different churches each Sunday meant that I never became part of a body, there was no personal involvement. So my commitment remained something between God and me. I'd no commitment to other people. I recognized quite clearly the need to go to church, arguing that if Jesus himself felt the need to go regularly to a place of worship, surely the same must be true for me.

I discussed this whole matter with various friends, including Roger, and listened to their advice. While I'd decided quite firmly not to return to the Catholic church, I was worried about upsetting my mother, who I knew would be unhappy about any change to another denomination. Very sensibly Roger advised me that I should join the local church wherever I happened to be living. That would make it easier to become involved in the activities of the fellowship, and get to know the other members. I agreed with him, and decided to wait until I was more settled before making a final decision. I wanted my choice to be a permanent one.

After working at the dentist's surgery for several months, the senior nurse, Sylvia, suddenly announced that she was getting married that Saturday. She certainly took everyone by surprise, as none of us even knew she had a fiance. She asked one of us to do her Saturday morning duty for her, as she'd forgotten to ask for the day off! I volunteered.

When I was alone in the surgery on that Saturday morning I realized that the temptation of working with drugs might one day prove too much for me, and I decided that I'd better resign before it was too late. It was a hard decision but I stuck to it even though I knew I'd probably be given Sylvia's job when she left.

I couldn't find another job that suited, so I considered going back into nursing. As I'd been absent for so long, however, I was told I would have to go back to prelims. That didn't appeal to me at all, and in any case I'd have the same temptation problem with nursing as with the dentist. But without a job, I couldn't afford to go on living in the flat. I was very unsure about what to do. Everything I'd done so far seemed to have been temporary, but I still wasn't sure that I had the confidence to plan a future for myself.

I went to see Roger and Margaret to ask their advice. They told me that they were going to move, as Roger had been appointed to a curacy in the west country.

'Would you like to move with us, Liesl?' they asked. 'A complete change of scene will probably help you a lot. And you can come back here now, then we can all make the move together.'

I was enormously touched that they should even consider taking me with them and very grateful that, yet again, they'd supported me through a difficult time. I was going to get right away from the drug scene, and, I hoped, from memories of mental illness. I'd be leaving all that behind me. A new life lay ahead.

22

FRESH START

Not long after the move, some of Roger's college friends arrived to stay — with the excuse that they were helping to redecorate the new home. At the time I wondered why I was being sent from one room to another to assist first Dick, then James, both of whom I'd already met. I was most impressed with how helpful and considerate they were! And it was only much later that I was told that they both loathed painting, but had come to see me, so Roger had arranged the painting rota accordingly. I was absolutely no good at that sort of painting — I wanted to get it all done much too quickly. And they didn't think much of my ideas for murals in all the rooms.

'We've got to live with it,' said Roger. 'No Liesl, not even one wall!'

It was an exhausting few days. When James invited me to go to the pub with him, I was glad of a break from the work but puzzled that he should find time to go out in the middle of it all. I had noticed his odd socks, and wondered whether he would change them before we went. He didn't. So, as we were walking along, I asked if he realized that he had odd socks on. In the middle of the street, he pulled his trousers up to his knees, looked down at his feet, and said calmly, 'Oh yes, so I have!'

'It's very good of you to help Roger and Margaret with the painting.' I commented. 'I hope they appreciate you both.'

'Oh, I can't stand painting,' admitted James. 'I hope we get it finished quickly.'

'Yes, it is rather boring,' I agreed, still not realizing what was going on.

When the job was done and James was leaving, he said that he'd like to see me again.

'But it will be at least three years before they re-paint,' I said.

He said he would write to me, and from then on our friendship developed and deepened.

The move and redecorating completed, I set about finding a job in the area. I saw an advertisement in the local paper for a post in a school for mentally handicapped children, and applied for it. I remember going to the interview in some trepidation, walking up the long drive to the school. I prayed as I walked that God would honour my decision to move right away from the drug scene and all its associations, and that he would help me to find the right job. As I got to the end of the drive, I realized that the school was attached to a hospital. I wondered what on earth I was doing applying for a job there. But I went on to the interview.

Mrs Wells, the supervisor of the Grange School, was a small, plump woman with dark hair. She took me into her office which was cluttered with books. I managed to fall over some boxes and by a stroke of good luck, landed on a chair.

'Well, that's a good start!' I thought.

'I usually fall over them as I'm going out,' Mrs Wells said cheerfully. 'I really must tidy up in here.'

She started to ask me the usual questions, such as where I lived and whether I'd worked with mentally handicapped children before.

'No I haven't,' I said.

'Why do you want to?' she asked.

'Because I've had some nursing experience, and I'd like to use it in some way.'

'Nursing training would be invaluable here,' she told me. 'This is a hospital school, and many of our pupils are rather low-grade. Spastics and other physically handicapped children do need a lot of nursing care.'

'What exactly do you mean by "hospital school"?' I wanted to know. She told me that the children were resident on the wards, and came across to school each day.

As she talked about the school, and its connection with the hospital, I felt I had to explain myself to her.

I told her that I hadn't completed my nursing training because I'd had a "bad nervous breakdown", and that the hospital treatment I'd received had got me addicted to drugs, and that I'd gone into the drug scene as a result.

'That's all in the past now,' I assured her, 'but I do feel it's important you should know. Also, I haven't had a long spell of working. But I'm sure I can handle a regular job now.'

She didn't make any comment at all, or show any reaction, but just went on to explain how the classes were arranged and so on. Then she asked me,

'Do you play the piano?'

'After a fashion.'

'That would be very useful for assembly.'

'Do you have assembly every day? And do the children get Bible teaching?' I asked.

'That's up to the teacher,' she said. 'The teaching programme is of necessity very flexible, because of the disabilities of these children. The work is largely nursing and supervision, so the term 'teacher' is a bit of a misnomer really. But to answer your question, we have an assembly every day when we sing simple hymns and have a story from the Bible.'

She showed me round the school, then took me into the staff-room for coffee and introduced me to the other members of staff. Then we went back to her office.

Without further ado, she said, 'I liked the way you spoke to the children. When can you start? Officially you'll be an assistant supervisor. I look forward to you starting as soon as possible.'

I was taken aback. I'd expected to be informed of her decision by a formal letter, not there and then!

'Oh, crumbs. Are you offering me the job?'

'Yes,' she said. 'I appreciated your honesty. A lot of people try to pull the wool over our eyes. Anyway, it sounds as though you might liven the place up!'

I could hardly believe it. I started work there the following Monday.

Finding a job committed me to staying in that area, and so the time had come to act on Roger's advice about joining a local church. But which one? All things considered, the Anglican church was the logical choice. I went up to Roger's study one evening to inform him of my decision.

'Roger, I've come to talk to you,' I announced.

'What! Again, Liesl?' He looked up from his cluttered desk. His cheerful, teasing manner was always in such contrast to the intense counselling I'd had in hospital. I found it easy to talk to him.

'I've decided I want to join the Anglican church. Do you think it's a good idea? Do I have to have instruction or a service or anything? Do I see you or the vicar about it? I feel a bit bad about my family, because I won't be able to explain to them, and I don't want them to be hurt. But I did decide ages ago that I wouldn't go back to the Catholic church. It seems like a good idea to make a fresh start.'

Roger put his pencil behind his ear and grinned.

'I'd like to have a receiving service or something,' I went on. 'Then at least I'll feel that I've really done something.'

'Don't you think it would be a good idea to sit down instead of propping up the door-post?' Roger enquired mildly. 'What do you expect me to say? You ask so many questions at once. Yes Liesl, I'm glad you've decided to join the Anglican church. Yes, I think you should do it formally, with a service. I can't tell you what you should do about your family. And why haven't you offered to make me some coffee?'

'Roger,' I complained, 'you're not taking me seriously. This is very important to me. How do I go about it?'

'Liesl, you come in here like a whirlwind, asking all these questions. I need coffee.'

So I went and made some, and took it to him.

'Curate, your coffee. Now, will you tell me how I go about arranging to have a service?'

Roger became practical then, and told me that I should go and see the vicar and discuss it with him. 'But of course they might not have you, Liesl,' he teased.

'Right, I'm off to see him now,' I replied. 'Shall I take him some coffee too?'

'Look,' said Roger, 'I'm going to be seeing him later on anyway. Would you like me to have a word with him first?'

'That's a good idea.'

So it was arranged. I had an interview with the vicar, who asked me how long I'd been a Christian and so on, and then in a short service one afternoon, with just the vicar and myself and Roger and Margaret present, I joined the Anglican church.

As we came out into the sunshine I remember thinking that I'd made a sensible move. I was relieved at having made the decision and carried it through for I saw it as a turning-point in my life. I was positively committing myself, not just to Jesus Christ but to other people. I realized that my decision carried an obligation to relate to other people, at least every Sunday, and that included strangers, which was a bit daunting. I hoped I'd have the self-discipline to sustain me.

I did still feel a bit guilty and worried about my family's reaction to the change. I decided not to tell them in order to avoid upsetting my mother, which meant attending the Catholic church whenever I was at home. I wondered how I'd feel about that, now I was an Anglican, but I came to the conclusion that God was everywhere, not confined to one denomination or one church, and I've held this belief ever since.

There were about a dozen children of different ages and types in my class at the Grange. The school catered for about fifty children altogether, most of whom lived in the hospital. I enjoyed my work very much and found it deeply satisfying. My first duty in the mornings was to collect the children from the wards, and help the nurses see that they got to school in good order. Then I'd help with, or lead, the assembly, often playing the piano.

I came to realize how much the children responded to music and singing, which was always a means of quietening them down if they got a bit out of hand in the classroom.

The children themselves were naturally affectionate, and it was a great joy to see each small improvement they made. One boy in particular stands out in my memory. Matthew was hyperactive as well as autistic. He'd been put up for adoption when he was a baby, but just before the adoption process was completed his condition was discovered, and so it all fell through. Ever since then he'd lived in the hospital, an exceptionally beautiful child, but always sad, never smiling. I discovered that if I looked at him when I spoke to him he would panic, but if I spoke while I was looking elsewhere, perhaps at someone else, but mentioning his name, he would respond and come close to me, sometimes hold onto my hand.

One day Jill, a little girl with Down's syndrome, was sitting on my knee. She was a jolly child, loving and co-operative, so I asked her to give me a smile which of course she did.

Then I said to her, but for Matthew's benefit, 'I'd like Matthew to give me a smile. One day he'll give us all a smile, won't he, Jill?'

Matthew came up to me and pushed Jill off my knee. I ignored him at first, just saying to Jill, 'Go and tell Mike that Matthew is going to give us a smile.' At that Matthew kissed me, and turned my face so that I had to look at him. He started smiling — and didn't stop. His smiles were infectious, and he became the joy of the whole school!

I often wondered what my attitude should be towards the possible 'healing' of these children, especially in the light of my own experience. But I certainly didn't have the confidence to suggest this in the staff room. I'd told the people there what had happened to me, and their comments had been, 'Oh, it's nice to have faith. You're one of the lucky ones.' 'Have you always been religious?' It worried me that they didn't take it seriously. To them it was just an interesting story, and the cost of telling it was that afterwards I felt that they looked sideways at me.

The question of healing and technology did come very much to the fore with the case of Lawrence, a four-year-old child with Down's syndrome who had a hole in his heart. He caught flu which developed into pneumonia. I went to visit him on the ward when he was too ill to come to school, and found him in an oxygen tent with drips and other life-support systems. He died soon after that.

I was amazed at the way the other children accepted his death. They were very positive about it, aware that Lawrence was no longer with them, and very loving in their recollections of him, going out of their way to try to say nice things. It struck me that, despite being in some cases severely subnormal, these children had a lot of love for one another.

Working in the school was very good for me. I was part of a team, which meant that I had to communicate with other members of staff. Even though there were tinges of a hospital institution, the system was very flexible: there was co-operation instead of pressure, and no feeling of anyone breathing down my neck. Above all, having to accept responsibility for myself and for others helped me a lot. And it taught me to have a sense of time again. In Mead Park and in Brooklands, time ceased to have any meaning, and punctuality was unimportant. But now I had to be at school at nine, and get the children ready for dinner by twelve o'clock, and back to the wards by four, and so on.

I made some new friends there, too. And there often seemed to be people, old student friends and others, dropping in at the Butlers' for coffee and a chat. I was still very much part of their home, and very grateful to them for all they'd done. We ate together in the evenings when I was there, but with an increasing social life I tended to see less and less of them.

Certainly picking up the threads of a normal life had its ups and downs. At first I used to get very tired with the day's work, and I realized that I was physically unfit. I tried playing tennis with friends, but I was so stiff the next day! It was always rather hard on my arms, and I was never able to enjoy it as I had before I was ill.

Most of my evenings were taken up with visiting friends, or writing to James, or going to the cinema. All these things were done with a special sense of newness and achievement. I was so aware of the progress I'd made.

I went to art classes, but not for very long. I soon decided that I was just wasting my money, as I was more inclined to observe the other would-be artists and the tutor than to concentrate on my own work. The tutor was a man of about seventy, with grey, wavy hair, a curly moustache and beady eyes. He was rather on the plump side, and I felt that braces might have been an asset! He was rather strange. It seemed that the only way he could actually teach us was by perching on a shooting stick. The moment he sat down his whole personality changed. The trouble was that the stick kept sliding across the slippery floor, to his extreme annoyance.

The other students were mostly older than me, very intense and solemn about what they were doing. They didn't seem aware of the tutor's eccentricities. I realized that I had a choice between taking it all seriously myself or leaving the class. My decision was made for me one evening when I did a cartoon of him instead of drawing the obligatory vase of flowers.

'Charcoal is a better medium for cartoons,' he commented drily.

For a while I continued to paint in the evenings, as it was a hobby which I enjoyed. But it aroused a feeling of conflict in me. It was a link with my old life and so, as I'd resolved to sever all such links, I decided to give it up.

23

THE ROAD TO FREEDOM

Life was good. Each day was a new day, a day free from psychiatrists and pills. I could make my own decisions free from supervision. I felt like a sort of Rip van Winkle, having been out of things for so long.

Before we moved to the west country, I'd been learning to cope with and adjust to everyday aspects of life, such as the changes of fashion, or slang. I'd been intrigued by such trivia as the amount of make-up women wore and the seeming vanity of visits to the hairdresser, for such things were far removed from my hospital life. I relished my new-found freedom in such matters as eating and sleeping, coming and going at will.

But now I moved into a deeper freedom. I was becoming a contributing member of society again. Hard as it was to believe at times, I was actually doing a responsible job, helping others instead of being a burden myself. I was working and mixing with people who, unless I chose to tell them, had no idea of what had happened to me. They accepted what they saw — a normal, cheerful person, not a write-off. I wondered sometimes whether this was perhaps a hypocritical position to be in. Had I a duty to explain? And I wondered, fearfully at times, whether this state of affairs, almost too good to be true, was a permanent one. I kept looking over my shoulder, comparing my life now with my position one, two, three years previously. Frequently I asked myself, 'Why me? Why did God choose to heal me?' Deeply conscious of the contrast between my old life and the new, I was constantly amazed at my own normality.

Of course there were difficulties, especially social ones. At parties I often felt awkward and at a disadvantage in conversations. I dreaded the usual questions: 'Where did you live before you came here? What did you do before you started at the Grange?' I had to avoid the issue, change the subject. There is so much stigma attached to mental illness.

Also I became aware of the abstract nature of many everday conversations — politics, the past, the future, ideas generally. In Brooklands any conversations we ever had tended to be selfish, self-centred, concerned only with one's own immediate needs and problems.

It was such a joy to me that each day I was a day further away from it all, a day further away from the nightmare, because of what God had done and was doing in my life. I knew that I'd never forget it all, and took great pleasure in wondering what the psychiatrists would make of my normal life, working with handicapped children, enjoying my freedom, in the light of their diagnosis of 'long-term patient . . . talking in terms of many years'.

Naturally, I was very sensitive about such remarks as 'Oh Liesl, you're nuts!' Of course I knew that they were meant to be taken lightly, just a figure of speech, but they struck home. Often I'd wonder, just for a moment, whether they really meant what they said. And I nearly always wondered when I got to know people whether I should tell them about myself. Ought I to explain, and would they understand?

I've always found, then and since, that reactions to my story are very varied. Comments like 'Oh well, all teenagers are screwed up anyway,' or 'Maybe you just pulled yourself together,' or 'Would you have been healed if you'd had cancer?' or 'It's all just another nutty experience,' were very hurtful. In any case they simply went against the facts of the case and proved that people hadn't heard or understood what I'd told them, or else hadn't been able to identify with it. If every teenager spent a considerable period of time in a locked room, or if every cure at the hands of the psychiatrists was an instantaneous one, then such remarks would have made sense.

On the other hand, I have been encouraged when people have responded positively and been helped by hearing my story.

One effect of negative attitudes was, and is, to make me very nervous of ever admitting to feeling the slightest bit 'low' for fear it might be interpreted as psychiatric depression. For instance, once I'd had bronchitis and as a result was a bit down. A friend refused to accept my explanation, saying that she thought perhaps 'Your psychiatric problems are coming back'. I found it impossible to accept the comparison between my slightly-less-than-cheerful attitude that evening and the depths of despair which had engulfed me when I was in Mead Park.

And certainly I wasn't depressed — life was too good for that! I knew I was no longer 'nuts', but I still found it difficult to cope with the memories of it all. I gradually came to realize that these were things which God would deal with in stages.

24

ROMANCE

During this time my friendship with James had deepened. He'd moved to be curate in a town a hundred miles away. Soon afterwards I started visiting him at weekends. His landlady, Mrs Perkins, was very good to us. She realized that I needed somewhere to stay and offered to put me up. She always made me most welcome.

At first I used to hitchhike, hoping that the weather wouldn't be too bad. But then one Saturday we went into town and I bought a small car with the money I'd got from selling my horse. It had been hard parting with Heidi. I'd had her since she was a foal, and she'd been kept for me at home all through my years in hospital. But I was obviously not able to keep her or ride her in a city, and a car was of much more use to me.

That car was a bit of a joke at the school, and it did let me down a few times. On one occasion, when I found myself without transport on a Friday afternoon, having planned to go and see James for the weekend, I went to a local car dealer after school and bought an old Austin for ten pounds. The driver's door didn't shut properly so it had to be tied with string and I climbed in through the window. I set off. I discovered to my cost that the petrol tank leaked, but I did manage to arrive safely.

As I arrived and parked in the drive, James came out to greet me. His face fell when he saw the car.

'What on earth have you got there?' he asked. 'It's quite ridiculous.'

It didn't help when I explained that I needed assistance to climb out through the window! He jokingly offered to repair the leak in the petrol tank for me — with chewing gum!

Somehow the car got me back home, where I sold it to another dealer for the same price I'd paid for it — ten pounds. And I kept the tax disc, thus making a small profit! Admittedly the dealer wasn't too enthusiastic about buying it, but I persuaded him that ten pounds was not an awful lot of money, as the car had just brought me over a hundred miles, so it couldn't be all that bad!

On another occasion I picked up a couple of hitchhikers. As we were travelling along, the car started to fill with smoke. Then the back seat began to smoulder. This was due, we discovered later, to the exhaust pipe chafing under the seat. I stopped the car, and we all got out and managed to smother the fire before it blazed up. At the time I was very impressed with how co-operative the hitchhikers were, not quite realizing, I suppose, the seriousness of a fire in a car! The crisis over, we continued our journey quite unperturbed!

One weekend James said, 'Come on, let's go down to Dorset next weekend. I'd like you to meet my parents.'

My immediate reaction was to say no, remembering my mother's comment, 'When he takes you home, wedding bells start to ring'. But eventually I agreed.

He picked me up after work one Friday in his 1928 Austin Seven — which he'd found in a chicken run during his student days and restored himself. I sat in the car for what seemed an endless drive, feeling very nervous, wondering what his parents would make of my visit. Would they preach at me? (I knew that James's father was a vicar.) How would they feel about an ex-Roman Catholic visiting their vicarage as a guest of their son? Naturally I wondered what James had told them about me and at the same time was concerned with the more trivial matter of whether I'd wake up in time for breakfast in the morning, as I was rather a heavy sleeper!

As we drove through a small village, James turned to me and said, 'It's not far now. About another twenty miles. We'll just call on some friends here as we're passing.'

I'd really had enough of the car journey and my apprehension was making me feel car-sick. The thought of visiting these unknown friends was just too much, and I said so.

'Don't worry,' said James 'We won't be long. Just a few minutes.' And he turned into a looped drive. As we arrived at the front of the house, two people came out to greet us. Strange, I thought, they didn't know we were coming, did they?

As I got out of the car James said with a grin, 'Meet my mother and father.'

I didn't know whether to be amused or annoyed at James's joke! But in the cheerful, comfortable atmosphere of the big, old-fashioned vicarage I soon relaxed. Hugh and Monica were very warm and welcoming and I was immediately impressed by the totally uncritical way they related to each other.

It was great to find that I didn't have to sit and make polite conversation. Hugh was very good at putting people at their ease, and over supper we all had a good laugh about James's little deception.

After the meal and helping with the washing up, we sat by the fire. I'd just taught myself how to crochet and had taken some work with me. I remember chatting to Monica about it, and explaining how I'd had to follow the instructions in front of a mirror, as they'd been intended for right-handed people, and I was left-handed!

Then I asked her what James had been like as a little boy. She said,

'Have a look at some photos of him, if you like.'

'Where are they?' asked James. 'I'll go and get them.'

He went off to fetch them from the sitting-room, and we sat and looked through pictures of the family at different ages and stages. Then I pulled a big photograph out of the pile. It was of a teenage boy talking to someone, surrounded by lots of old watches.

'Oh no, that wasn't you, was it?' I asked.

'Yes, it's me,' he said.

'That wasn't you on the television, was it?' I asked again.

'Yes,' he said. 'But how did you know it was on television?'

I couldn't believe it. The boy with the collection of watches. I remembered it all so clearly — watching television at home in the library, my father asleep in his chair, my amazement that someone of fifteen should have had such a fascinating hobby, and how I'd wondered if I might meet him. What a coincidence!

The other thing I remembered being impressed by was how calm and controlled he'd seemed.

'Were you nervous?' I asked.

'No, I thought it was all rather fun,' he said in his unruffled way.

'Have you still got all those watches?'

'Yes. Do you want to come and have a look?' James took me to his extraordinary room. There were pieces of clocks and watches on every available surface. And thirteen clocks, all chiming!

After that weekend I met Hugh and Monica quite frequently when they were visiting James's grandmother and uncles. It was of course difficult for us to go to Dorset at the weekends as James's duties tied him to the church. A weekly pattern emerged for me, working at the Grange from Mondays to Fridays, then straight after school driving the hundred miles to spend the weekend with James.

Over the months we visited all the local places of interest — stately homes, museums and old church towers, always ending up back at Mrs Perkins' house in time for tea before the drive back home on Sunday evening ready for the next week's work.

25

A PROPOSAL

One weekend we were up yet another church tower, looking around. It was cold and I sat down, shivering, but James started clearing up the pigeon muck.

'What on earth are you doing?' I asked. 'Do come and sit down.'

But he continued, commenting at the same time that it was disgusting that the place was in such a condition. Eventually, when it was tidied to his satisfaction, he came and sat next to me.

'How would you like to be married to a curate?' he enquired.

'No curate's ever asked me,' I replied.

'There's one asking you now,' he said.

I was somewhat taken aback. I managed to say something like, 'Oh, I don't know. I can't think here among all this mess.'

This had really not been my vision of a proposal. Where were the soft lights and the music, the dinner with wine and candles and red roses?

James didn't seem to worry that he hadn't had a direct answer. The next evening he simply said,

'When shall we announce our engagement? What about your birthday?'

'Are you serious?' I asked. 'Can you really put up with me for the next sixty years?'

'I think so,' he said. 'In fact, I haven't been able to "put up" without you for the last two weeks since that silly argument we had. They've been the worst two weeks of my life. But perhaps it was a good thing in a way — it made me realize how much I love you!'

'Yes, I agree. I felt the same,' I said.

So when Mrs Perkins came in with some cocoa for us, he said that we'd something to tell her.

'We're getting engaged,' he announced.

She was very excited about it, and immediately decided that we must celebrate with a glass of sherry. Of course she wanted to know when we'd be getting married, and what about the ring, and so on.

After she'd left us, James asked me what sort of ring I wanted. A red one, I decided. Would we choose it together?

'You can choose it yourself, if you like,' he volunteered.

'No, let's go together,' I said, amused at his practical matter-of-fact attitude.

When it came to it, of course, neither of us had any money, so we decided to look around the second-hand shops, which always seemed to have a better selection of clocks than rings! James's attention constantly wandered from the task in hand to his interest in the make and movements of the various clocks on display. Finally we found what we wanted in a little shop run by a short, plump woman of about sixty, with peroxide blonde hair and a bright blue streak down the middle of the parting! She was wearing masses of beads, a ring on every finger, bright red lipstick, and so much powder that I was sure I could have blown it off her nose!

And after all that, James wouldn't let me keep the ring until my birthday and the official engagement. By which time of course he'd braved my father, to ask for his permission to marry me. To that question James received the brisk retort, 'It's no good asking me. Ask her!'

Life became a busy round of work and wedding preparations, and of buying bits and pieces for our future home. One of our purchases was a four-poster bed which belonged to a friend of my mother's. She was rather reluctant to sell it, but after a lot of persuasion agreed to let us have it for sixty pounds. The deal concluded, we suddenly realized that there was no way we could get it out of her house. We had to take it completely to pieces, then lower the bits out of the window into the bushes. As the garden was rather over-grown, a bit like Sleeping Beauty's castle, it wasn't easy. But eventually we managed to load it up and get it back to James's village, where we placed it gently in the eighteenth-century church cottage which was to be our future home.

Most of our time at weekends now seemed to be spent on visits to sale rooms, and on re-painting — the practice we'd had on Roger and Margaret's home no doubt helped!

26

A WEDDING IN WALES

My own happiness didn't prevent me from feeling sad at leaving the Grange. Working there had been such a positive experience for me. I'd grown very fond of the children, and there were tears as well as good wishes all round at my leaving party. The next day I went home to Wales with the wedding only a week away.

When I arrived everything seemed to be in some confusion. Because of my mother's state, there had been mix-ups over invitations. Some had still not even been sent, but were on the dining-room table, along with other wedding paraphernalia and a typewriter with my mother's uncompleted book. She was drunk and my father greeted me with 'What the hell are you doing here?' in his usual gruff but affectionate way.

'I've come home to get married, and to give a hand with the preparations,' I replied.

'Oh,' he said. 'Well, does that fuzzy-haired chap know what he's taking on?'

'I don't know, but I don't think I'll tell him at this stage!' I answered.

When James phoned that night I told him, 'There's chaos here. I don't know what's going on.'

'I don't suppose it matters,' he replied re-assuringly.

I was worried too because my dress was still not finished. I'd designed it myself, in an Edwardian style, and Margaret was making it for me. James was planning to wear a frock-coat, which he'd bought in the Portobello Road market in London, and he had Georgian silver buckles for his shoes.

That night my mother became delirious, trying to persuade me to phone Prince Charles about something she decided she had to tell him. I managed eventually to get her to go to bed, and phoned the doctor, who came and gave her an injection to sedate her. I sat with her for the rest of the night, wondering how I was ever going to sort everything out. I tried to explain to my family that I couldn't cope, and by the time James phoned the next evening I was almost ready to go along with his suggestion that if things got too bad, we could get married in his parish. That of course would have meant that my family couldn't be there, and I did so much want it to be a family occasion.

By the wedding day itself, everything was amazingly organized and calm. I remember walking across the red flagstones to the kitchen, seeing the piles of newspaper where the dogs had puddled in the night, and thinking, 'This is my wedding-day.'

My father was in the kitchen with Margaret and Helga, and I said to them, 'I'm off to the hairdresser.'

My father asked, 'What on earth for? What's going on? What are all these people doing?'

'I'm getting married today,' I reminded him.

'What! Today? Next week isn't it?'

'For goodness' sake,' I exclaimed. 'I'm your youngest daughter, and you forget the day of my wedding!'

'I don't know,' he grumbled. 'Nobody tells me anything in this house. Oh well, I'll get you off my hands a week earlier than I'd expected.'

Then before I could get away to the hairdresser

— complete, on my mother's insistence, with the family tiara — Margaret wanted me to try my dress on, so that she could finish the hem. She pinned it all, pleating the ruffles, at the same time reassuring me that it would be done in time. In the event, she was still putting the finishing touches to it and cutting odd threads, as I got into the car with my father to go to the church!

From that moment on, everything went beautifully. It was a lovely wedding, an occasion of great happiness — and one or two amusing hiccups. On the way home from the church our journey was interrupted from time to time by local children holding tapes or ribbons across the road. Custom demanded that we stop and throw pennies to them before driving through the ribbons. Needless to say, the car had been well stocked with coins in readiness for this. But at one such stop the horn jammed, so James, in his wedding finery, had to get out and scrabble around under the bonnet. It was a vintage car so no one else had a clue how to disconnect the horn.

We planned to spend that night in the flat in the grounds, as the house and all the local hotels were full of family and friends. On our arrival at the flat we found the place full of camp-beds and suitcases belonging, I discovered, to various young friends. They'd needed somewhere to stay! We crept back into the house while the guests were still enjoying the barbecue. We phoned a friend, who agreed to put us up.

I'd had the usual romantic ideas about where I wanted to go for my honeymoon — somewhere exotic with palm trees and moonlight and so on. Alternatively, I would really have liked to go to Iceland! Our finances didn't run to either of those options, so when someone in the next parish offered us the loan of his lodge on a small Scottish island, we gratefully accepted.

It was a large house, very comfortable and peaceful, even if not quite what I'd envisaged. I felt horribly seasick on the way across from the mainland. When we arrived, everyone on the island was very friendly. Knowing that we were on honeymoon, they treated us so warmly that it was like an extension of our wedding-party; they celebrated with us, never treating us as outsiders. We were invited to dinner, and taken to a ceilidh.

And then, one day, one of the islanders brought us a live lobster as a gift. I refused to do the murder. As the wretched thing started to crawl towards me, I leapt onto a chair in the kitchen, saying to James,

'If this is married life, I'm not sure I want it!'

He just walked out of the kitchen saying, 'This is your department.'

'Don't be unreasonable,' I protested. 'I thought you promised to look after me.'

He eventually dealt with the lobster, and I made him agree that if this particular item was ever on the menu again, he would be chief cook!

27

WORKING TOGETHER

'We had rather a lot of boiled eggs!' said James recently when I asked him to recall our early married life. 'And you did have difficulty waking up in the mornings, however loudly I played the piano.'

'Well, you certainly managed to disturb me with your keep-fit exercises,' I countered. 'And what about the time you were sleep-walking and started giving a sermon out of the window?'

Of course, there were the usual adjustments that every young couple has to make, but from the beginning we felt that we should work together as a team. James had firmly rejected the idea that I find a job, insisting that he wanted me to be in the home and in the parish.

So I set about getting to know people, shopping in the local shops, making use of my nursing experience whenever the need arose, and chatting to the young people who stood aimlessly on street corners with nothing to do. We invited people into our home, and tried to help in whatever way we could. We wanted to share our own happiness and enthusiasm with those around us. Sometimes we played practical jokes, such as the time we walked through the town together, James's head covered by a large paper bag, while I asked passers-by,

'Oh, I wonder if you could help me. My husband's got his head stuck in this bag!'

Another time James found some tourists wandering in our garden. When they asked him if we were open to the public he charged them two shillings each and showed them round, indicating that I was the maid!

I got involved with the church stall for the local market. A group of us spent an enjoyable evening each week making toys such as matchbox furniture, football badges and Indian head-dresses — for which I collected feathers from local farms and dyed them. It was a very good way of getting to know people and making money for the church at the same time.

After a while our home became a 'coffee stop' with all sorts of people dropping in — from bored teenagers to middle-aged housewives, couples with problems, or those who were just plain lonely. We loved being able to open our home to them, working together to try to help.

At one time or another we had various people staying with us. Jeffrey was one such guest. He was about seventeen, very unhappy at home, and had started to dabble in drugs. He needed a lot of time and care and counselling, but when he left us after a couple of weeks to return home, he was fine and kept in touch with us until we moved on.

I found his case in particular very encouraging, for here I was helping someone with a drug problem, even though a minor one. It made me see clearly how much my life had changed. And I couldn't help but smile sometimes at my own dilemma over which church I should join when I was living with Roger and Margaret. Now I was not only a member of the Anglican church, but I was actually working within it.

In the midst of all this I became pregnant. The

village seemed to share in our excitement at the birth of our daughter, Emily, and motherhood opened the door to contact with other young mothers, giving me the opportunity to visit them in their homes. I always felt that we couldn't expect people to come to church if they didn't know what they were coming to and who they would meet there.

Parish life was good, but we found that as we got more involved and drew closer to people there were deeper needs, and we realized that we were rather ineffective in dealing with these. As we became increasingly aware of this lack of power and frustrated by our inability to convey the reality of God and his purposes, we knew there was something missing.

One day I was discussing this and other personal matters with a close friend. He mentioned that he had been to a Christian conference the previous year.

'Believe me, Liesl, it was not at all like normal conferences. I went there in a rather depressed frame of mind, and it helped me considerably. Everyone was so filled with enthusiasm for their faith, and it certainly added a new dimension to mine — it opened my eyes to a more personal relationship with God, especially in helping people in the course of my work. I think you should both go this year. Why don't you?'

'Oh, no!' I thought. 'Ian may have enjoyed it, but all those meetings and discussion groups sound too much like group therapy to me!'

A few days later Ian called to see James and again suggested that we go to the conference. James said politely that he would think about it, but I was sure that he wasn't at all keen. No doubt he had a mental image of a dull and dry clergy conference!

But Ian didn't let the matter rest there. He overrode our objections about not being able to afford it, and not having a suitable car for the journey, by offering us the use of his car and insisting on paying for us to attend. We felt that we could not refuse, so with some trepidation we set off for the conference centre.

From the moment we arrived we were struck by the atmosphere. These people had something different — a freedom, a power, an authority, which came from God. Here were people who lived their lives by taking God at his word, trusting him to deal with their problems, and taking it for granted that he would help and heal those who turned to him. These were not 'special' people — they were all quite ordinary.

The talk that evening was about the power of the Holy Spirit, and on how it applied to the church today with the same relevance as in the days of the early church: how the power to heal the sick, to perform miracles, to speak in unknown tongues, to preach with authority, and to cast out demons — in fact, all the aspects of Christ's ministry — was available today, just as it had been made available to the disciples on the Day of Pentecost.

'But the trouble is that too many of us try to do things in our own strength. That is futile, when God is willing to give us his infinitely greater strength to help us do his work. For example, a man may be trained as a carpenter, and may become a proficient one, but he is useless without tools. Have we got the tools of our trade as Christians?'

I knew that I'd personally experienced the

miraculous power of God in my life, but it had seemed an almost isolated occurrence, abnormal, out of the realm of everyday Christian living. Yet here was someone presenting the picture of miracles, healings and so on as the normal way God wants to work through his church and through each and every individual in the church. I recognized the simplicity and the uncomplicated truth of what he said.

It all made sense. This was what we lacked.

He continued, 'If you're feeling ineffective as a Christian; if you're seeking this gift, this free gift from God, come forward and we'll pray for you, and lay hands on you.'

Both James and I went forward. I remember wondering what was going to happen, and what I would do if James received this gift and I didn't.

Afterwards, it was suggested that we simply go away and pray without worrying about the words we used, 'Just carry on, don't worry about feeling silly,' he said. James and I went and sat together in a small alcove downstairs. I hadn't felt very much when I'd been prayed for, but I was glad I'd gone forward. I asked James what he thought, and he answered calmly that he believed he'd been released into the power of the Holy Spirit, even though he hadn't felt anything either. Then we prayed together, holding hands as a sign of our working together in God's ministry. As we did so, we knew that God had answered our prayer, for we both started praying in tongues — words we didn't know, just a few words at first, later to become more fluent.

We felt very relaxed and at the same time excited. We were filled with an inexpressible joy, and a real confidence that this was the normal

Christian life, the answer to deadness in so many churches.

We phoned Ian to share with him what had happened.

'That's great,' he said. He sounded really excited too. 'I just knew you would benefit from going. I'm so glad I was able to persuade you. You were so reluctant at first!'

Over the next few days, we found a new expectancy about how God would use us to help other people and a new confidence that he would supply our needs, and other people's. There was a new reassurance that we could now offer the gospel with power, and not just with words and knowledge. We were in a state of euphoria; life had taken off in an even more exciting direction. We were equipped with 'the tools of our trade' and it was going to be up to us to put them to use.

Looking back on our remaining days in that town, we see that it was a time of training, an apprenticeship, a working out together of how Jesus intended his people, the church, to live — effectively and powerfully.

All in all those years were a time of stability, of happiness and of learning to work together as a team.

But the time came to think of moving on.

James wrote to his old Cambridge college, but received no reply. It was about a year later — by which time James had applied for and considered various other posts — that there arrived in the mail one morning a letter from the Dean, apologizing for his oversight in not having answered James's letter. He supposed that it was now too late, but he told us that there was a job going in a village in the east of the country, and he wondered if we were still interested. So he was writing on the off-chance.

As James read out the letter I just knew that this was where we would be going, and James obviously felt the same. We knew this was from God — in his timing.

Everything about the move seemed to fall into place. So, with a small daughter, a once-again-dismantled four-poster bed, and a sense of anticipation, we moved to our new parish.

28

A NORMAL LIFE

Full of enthusiasm and ideas — God's ideas — we made the move. We found a somewhat run-down church building which needed a lot of repairs and a small congregation which had been kept together by a loyal few. It was a great challenge and we plunged into it immediately.

Our first priority was to get the church on the map within the local community, and this involved an enormous amount of visiting. We started on this at once, almost before we'd arranged the furniture and hung the curtains.

From the nucleus of a well-attended Sunday school we were put into contact with older brothers and sisters and so came into existence our first youth group. And after Christmas we started a small Bible study group. By the end of our first year — at which time our second daughter, Iona, was born — we were running four different groups.

My time was constantly divided between my family and the parish. Combining my 'vicar's wife' role with being a mother has always been interesting. I'm very conscious that clergy wives can all too easily get so involved with parish work that they neglect their own children.

So my days were full and varied — visiting between feeding times; serving coffee to the distraught and doubting while peeling potatoes; answering the telephone and loading the washing machine; helping with homework on the one hand and handing out advice on domestic problems on the other.

When someone came to the door, he or she might stay for five minutes, or for several weeks! When callers came with medical problems they could simply have heard on the grapevine that I'd been a nurse, or they could be seeking prayers for help or healing.

Over the years James enrolled the church and the village in a labour force to deal with the necessary restoration work on the church, thus cutting the cost considerably. I was usually coffee-maker-in-chief to these work parties, which were cheerful occasions, drawing people closer together.

As more people have joined our fellowship, we've seen them in their turn give their time and talents to helping others. Concerts and celebrations have drawn the village into the church, and participation in village events has made the church more recognized as a real and vital part of the village.

Being a vicar — or a vicar's wife — can never be a nine-to-five job. Our home is our office, and the scene of many of our church activities.

It's an exciting life. Of course there are downs as well as ups, failures as well as successes. But the joy of seeing a former atheist come to church, the enthusiasm of children who discover that God really does answer their prayers, the gratitude of those who've been helped in some way, the clear evidence of God's power shown through some occasions when we've prayed for healing — these for me are an essential and integral part of the normal Christian life.

29

OFFER OF RELEASE

Against this background of a normal and fulfilling life, there is still one area of my life which is not easy to talk about. I find it provokes strong reactions.

Also, it means backtracking some years in my story. For even as a Christian, life had not been smooth and untroubled. There was in fact an explanation of why my life had so many unusual difficulties and struggles, and this I must somehow try to share with you.

I have been made aware, not only of the power of God, but of the power of that great enemy of God, the spiritual power of evil, Satan himself. Perhaps my own case was an extreme one. But we must never lose sight of the fact that the cause of so many problems can be the one whose whole aim is to undermine and spoil God's work.

The story that follows, which has deliberately been kept out of sequence, looks back to another, very different experience of God's power, a far greater power than Satan's.

Various facts about my infancy, previously unknown to me, came to light in the course of the week I am about to describe. These facts were subsequently checked and found to be true.

At that time I was generally cheerful and leading a normal life. But sometimes when I went to church,

I'd burst into tears without warning and have to leave. I wasn't actually sad about anything in particular, but just conscious of being weighed down by a blanket of sorrow. On occasions this also descended on me when I was praying. It seemed as though there was something deep within me which was unhappy about the turn my life had taken, and would like to force me backwards again. I felt very bad about this negative emotion, and about having to walk out of church, because I knew that God had done so much for me.

I tried to carry on, telling myself that all was well, but as I tried to move forwards, I was conscious of being tugged backwards — a tug-of-war that seemed interminable. On the whole I was enjoying my life, but I suddenly started waking up at night with a feeling of chill going through me, followed by a sensation of panic. At times it was so bad that I almost fainted, or I was so scared that I dared not move even a limb. Then I would vomit and shake violently. Sometimes it all lasted for about an hour, at other times only for a few minutes, and I found that praying helped considerably. I was always fine the next morning so there seemed no point in going to a doctor.

I suppose that I must have realized by then that perhaps there was something wrong which was beyond my control, a spiritual problem that I needed help with.

I went to see Mr Jones, a Congregational minister, because I'd heard that he helped people with problems and struggles. He was a warm, friendly man, obviously very competent. He explained that he used to work with a team and that some of his friends were coming to stay, so he invited me to meet them.

I called one evening as arranged, having decided that I wouldn't tell them anything. For some reason I didn't want to reveal my past — talking about it was something I've always found difficult.

They sat me down and started asking me questions.

'We understand that you're a Christian, Liesl?'

'Yes,' I replied.

'You see, we don't minister in this way to non-Christians,' the man went on.

'What do you mean by "this way"?' I wanted to know.

So he explained that God wants us to be whole, but Satan does all he can to destroy that wholeness. God's power, however, is far greater than Satan's.

Then he asked me what my problem was.

I was still reluctant to give them my whole history, so I just told them about my difficulties with sleeping and with dreams, and said that I felt there was a block in my Christian life.

'Well, we really don't know anything about you Liesl, but do you believe what the Bible says, that "Satan goes round like a roaring lion, seeking whom he may devour"?'

'Yes,' I agreed.

'Is it possible that there have been incidents in your life which might have provided an open door to Satan?'

'What do you mean exactly?' I queried.

'Well, for example, someone brought up in an atmosphere of fear or violence, which sometimes goes back to childhood, has a door opened to a "spirit of fear".'

'Well, I've had a nervous breakdown,' I admitted, 'and there have been various other problems which I don't want to go into now, but could that explain the block?'

'Yes, it could. God's will is for us to be free but perhaps these problems have allowed Satan to get a hold on you. I suggest we pray, but before we do, let's ask Frank to come in. He's a member of our team who has a gift of knowledge. Do you understand what I mean by a gift of knowledge, Liesl?'

I said that I did. I'd read about it in the Bible: it was one of the gifts of the Holy Spirit. But I had no personal experience of it.

Then they prayed.

For some reason that made me terribly angry and I felt that I could have hit them. I know that I was very impatient and irritable, and I didn't understand what was happening. But they just carried on talking to me and praying. In fact, they spent many hours with me. I was extremely depressed, somehow aware of a deep spiritual darkness within me, almost threatening to smother the light.

When they stopped praying they said they felt that the whole group should pray with me and invited me to go to stay with members of their team.

'How do you feel about that?' they asked.

'OK, but puzzled about what it would involve.'

'You'd have to stay with them for a few days. We feel that Satan has a deep grip on your life, and it would be wise for you to be completely under their care, so that they'll be able to support you as necessary.'

When they talked of the home as being a healing centre and told me of several cases of people bound by Satan in different ways finding freedom through their ministry, I felt reassured.

I rang the number they'd given me and made arrangements to go and stay with them.

30

WAITING FOR RELEASE

I travelled by train and was met at the station by Mary. Tall and with a lively face, she was a gentle, confident person, full of fun and, as I discovered later, very fond of music. I was nervous, wondering how much I should tell them, and very reluctant to go through my whole history. I also felt very embarrassed that they were putting themselves out so much for me. I found it hard to accept their loving, considerate concern. I was frightened that they'd think that I wasn't a Christian. After all, it did seem odd for a Christian to have such struggles.

With these thoughts swirling through my head we arrived at the house. It was quite large and had a small garden facing onto a wide road, just a few minutes' walk from some shops. The lawn was scattered with children's toys, and there was a swing in one corner. Mary took me inside and I was introduced to Jackie and her children, and to the other members of the household. Then we had tea.

After tea I wasn't quite sure what to do and rather hoped that they would pray with me that evening. But when nothing happened I wished that I had brought some knitting or something to do. Then Mary made some tea and suggested that we went together into the other room for a chat. After we'd chatted for a while, she asked me to tell her a bit about myself.

'Well I feel that there's a block in my Christian

life,' I said. 'I don't know if there's a connection between that and my nervous breakdown.'

'Are you fully recovered from your breakdown?' Mary asked me.

'Yes, I am. But it has obviously scarred me.'

'People who come to us have various problems,' Mary explained. 'Some are seeking healing and many are bound or in some way possessed by Satan. But it is very exciting to see God freeing these people through the ministry of prayer.'

Her attitude seemed very positive and I asked her, 'Do you think I am possessed?'

'Well, there's clearly something blocking your Christian life, as you put it, and that's certainly not from God and not what he wants for you. We'll be praying with you, and seeking God's guidance. But don't worry. There's nothing to fear. God is stronger than Satan. We can trust God completely and because we're Christians we know that Jesus Christ defeated Satan in his victory on the cross.'

This new approach excited me but I felt apprehensive. Mary and I chatted generally for a while. In the course of the conversation, she asked me if I played the piano and told me I was welcome to play hers any time I liked.

I went to bed, but couldn't sleep; thoughts of what to say, and where to start, and how much to tell them kept going round and round in my head. Everyone seemed so relaxed, and I began to think that I was just being silly, that they'd never understand anyway, and I didn't want to have to explain to them the details of my time in psychiatric hospitals. I ended up wishing that I hadn't gone there at all.

The next morning, when I went down to breakfast, they told me that they had someone else coming to see them that morning, and so they'd see me later in the day. I was disappointed, but I decided to go and get some wool to knit a jumper — I remember that I bought blue. As I walked along I thought about the delay, and I couldn't help wondering just when something was going to happen. What a waste of time!

When I got back to the house, I still didn't know quite what to do with myself. Where should I sit? Where were they going to see this other person? Could I play the piano now, or would that disturb them? What was the other person coming about anyway? If they were going to be busy, should I offer to look after the children, or should I wait for them to ask me?

I sat down in the sitting-room with my wool and started knitting. Jackie brought in some coffee. She sat down and chatted while she did some mending, and the children played. She asked me about myself, so I told her that I used to nurse, but that I hadn't completed my training. Naturally she asked me why that was, so I just said that I'd been ill, and didn't pursue the conversation further. Neither did she.

While we were talking Jackie kept going to answer the phone, and once she left me alone for a while to put some clothes into the washing machine. When she came back into the room, she told me that she had to go out to take one of the children somewhere, so would I mind answering the phone? I was just to say that John and Mary were tied up, but that they'd ring back.

As I sat there, again not quite sure what to do, I heard voices from the next room raised in prayer. Suddenly there was a blood-curdling screech. It sounded so frightening, so evil. I wondered what on earth was going on. Why didn't the visitor leave? I didn't associate the screech with him. I was upset by it, but what should I do? Should I stay sitting there or should I go for a walk and get out of the way?

Jackie came back, having left her child playing with friends. There was silence next door, but of course I wanted to know what had been going on, and what the screech had been.

Jackie just put her head round the door. 'I'm back,' she said. 'John and Mary are still tied up, are they?'

'Yes, they are,' I replied. I desperately wanted to ask her about what was going on, but felt too scared by what I'd heard.

Then the door-bell rang, while I was still deciding what to say. Jackie let in a woman who came and sat down in the sitting-room with me. She seemed to know where everything was, so she must have been there before. I learned that she was the visitor's wife, and that she'd come to pick him up. I considered telling her what I'd heard, then decided that it wasn't really my business.

Soon after that he came into the sitting-room with John and Mary. He looked radiant, full of joy, and I was totally puzzled. How could I reconcile what I was seeing now with what I'd heard a short while ago?

'Oh, Bill! You do look better,' exclaimed his wife. And she put her arms round him.

Bill sat down, saying, 'I'm feeling a bit dazed actually.'

Then Mary said that they'd had a good morning, and that Bill had been helped a lot. They all chatted cheerfully for a few minutes before Bill and his wife left.

I still wanted to ask about the screech, but thought that as it had been a private consultation, I'd better not. But over lunch, Mary and John were expressing their happiness about Bill's 'deliverance'. I turned to Mary and said, 'I heard an awful screech.'

'Yes, I thought perhaps you'd heard it. I hope you weren't too upset by it, because it wasn't really disturbing. It's marvellous to see the power of God over Satan.'

And John said, 'It's very clear in the Bible, you know, that there were disturbances when spirits were cast out. For instance, in Mark's Gospel when Jesus commanded the evil spirit out of the man in the synagogue it says, "The evil spirit shook the man violently and came out of him with a shriek". There is usually some manifestation but it is not always so dramatic. It's sometimes just a sigh or a slight shiver. But the person concerned is always aware of a sense of release.'

I wanted to ask a lot of questions like, 'Did Bill feel scared at the time?' and 'Does it always work?' I couldn't understand why I hadn't heard about all this before; after all, I'd read the Gospel stories. Why hadn't I registered that 'casting out demons' was part of Jesus' ministry just as 'healing the sick' was? From my experience, I was very aware that healing was as relevant today as it had been two thousand years ago, so the same must be true of everything else.

But I still felt very uncomfortable about it all. I kept thinking, 'I'm going! I'm leaving here!' I wanted to go, but at the same time I felt that I had to stay.

I was still wondering whether to go or stay as I did the dishes. Jackie's little boy was standing on a stool next to me, doing the drying. Like most young children, he was observant and direct. He saw the scars on my arms and asked me about them. 'I had an accident,' I replied.

Immediately I'd said it I realized that I'd lied to him, a child in a Christian household. I felt very guilty and it was clear to me that I'd have to decide on a fair answer to that question which came up over and over again. It was — and still is — a sensitive subject for me.

31

RELEASE FROM FEAR

I stood at the sink, my thoughts in a whirl. What was going to happen to me? When would it happen? Should I go, or should I stay?

I was still considering the whole matter when John came into the kitchen and made up my mind for me by saying, 'Liesl, would you like to come and sit down with us in the other room?'

I felt terrified. I went into the room thinking that I just couldn't bear to go over my whole past. It was no good. There was no way that I could talk about it all. I told them so, but they assured me that they were there to help me, and I should talk just as and when I wanted to.

'But I can't, I feel terrified,' I said.

'Well, let's talk about the fear then.'

They asked me questions: 'Have you felt like this before?' 'Do you often feel like this?' 'Are there certain situations which make you frightened?' 'Or do you suddenly feel like this with no obvious explanation?'

Then came the question I'd been expecting ever since I arrived.

'How did you become a Christian?' asked John.

I explained that at three o'clock one morning I had come to the conclusion that Jesus was on the outside of my life, and so I'd asked him to come and be on the inside.

Mary then said that they felt the way to handle the problem was to start by asking God to show them how to help me. They sat me on a chair, and told me that they would pray as God led them. I was to relax, they said.

As they started to pray a knot of fear formed in my stomach. It slowly moved up to my chest and became quite painful. Every now and again they would stop praying and talk to me. They explained that at some point in my life, fear had found an entry, and that they were going to command it out of me.

'Do you understand, and are you happy about that?' John asked.

'Yes,' I replied, for I felt secure in their handling of the situation. They assured me that God had victory over all things, including fear, and that Jesus had come to set people free. They continued praying, one of them praying in tongues, and suddenly I had a choking sensation and started to shake uncontrollably. I shook so badly that I had difficulty staying on my chair. I can only explain it by saying that I had all the physical sensations of fear, but no emotional sensation as I'd had in the past. I wondered how long the shaking would continue. Then I coughed and instantly felt a great sense of relief. The shaking subsided. Then I heard John saying that while he'd been praying, God had given him a picture of a big house with a parapet over the porch.

He continued, 'He's also given me a picture of a portrait. The eyes in that painting are of great concern to you. Somehow that was an opening for fear, which has been a consistent emotion in your life.'

They prayed together again, then John asked if his comments had meant anything to me.

'There was a painting like the one you describe,'

I told him. 'It was in the dining-room at home. The most noticeable thing about it was the eyes. They seemed to watch and follow you, wherever you were in the room. My mother was very proud of it, and used to show off the 'moving eyes' to visitors, but it terrified me, especially when I had to be alone in the room practising the piano. At one time the piano was moved so that my back was to the picture but I was so upset that I refused to play at all. I suppose that it was childish imagination, but that picture certainly did have a big effect on me.'

'Was that your home — the house with the parapet which I saw?' asked John.

'Yes,' I answered.

'How did you feel about the house?' Mary asked me.

'I was always frightened in it,' I admitted.

They asked me to tell them more about the house, how long I'd lived there and so on, and whether my family had known about my fears.

'They always put it down to my being a tiresome child,' I explained.

Mary said, 'There is a great deal of fear in that house.'

They continued praying about fear.

As they prayed, I burst into tears and shouted, 'It's haunted! It's haunted!'

They both just said, 'Yes.'

I was really excited and encouraged when I realized that they did believe me. They weren't just humouring me, and I didn't have to try to convince them, because they knew and understood. There had been such authority in that 'Yes'.

They prayed against the effects that the house had had on me, along with the hurt I'd felt in not being believed and understood as a child.

I remember thinking, 'Well, that's great, that's all cleared up now.' But John said that he felt they should continue to pray, and I thought, 'Oh dear. We'll never get to anything else if we take so long over this fear business.'

My body felt battered, as if it had been under prolonged strain. I suppose it was the same sort of feeling as when you've been ill, and the aches and pains go, leaving you exhausted but relieved that the illness has gone. I just sat there while they prayed. Then John asked me if there was a lot of land attached to the house, and Mary said that she had a picture of some water, perhaps a pond or a lake, and that she knew it was connected with my fear in some way.

'It isn't clear. Can you explain it?' Mary asked. 'I just know that there was water and a lot of fear attached to it.'

So I told them about my father and his walled garden.

'I had to go past a small lake if I wanted to go to that garden, you see, but it terrified me. I'd no idea why at the time, but after I left home I heard a rumour that many years previously the body of a man who had died in mysterious circumstances had been thrown into the lake.'

So they prayed about the emotional strain caused by that fear separating me from my father.

Then we talked for a while and had a cup of tea. As we chatted, I began to feel far more at ease. I realized that God was certainly showing them things very accurately and so I felt able to trust them more fully. I felt more free to talk about myself and decided to tell them that I'd had a bad breakdown, that my mother was an alcoholic, and of the circumstances of my healing. I wondered whether I should even tell them of my involvement with drugs and with palmistry.

As I relaxed a little I asked them why I'd shaken so much when they prayed. They explained again that fear had taken a grip on my life, and that the shaking was simply a sign of it leaving. They said that in order to recognize these things, the spiritual gift of discernment was needed.

I felt relieved to be free of the fear but they warned me that they felt I needed a lot more ministry. I might have to stay for a whole week, they said, for they were going to pray in stages. They were extremely positive about it all and were very excited that God had brought me so far, and that he was doing so much in my life. In spite of their encouragement I felt depressed. I hadn't expected it to be a long drawn-out thing — after all, when I'd been healed there had just been a few prayers and it was all over. I suppose I'd hoped for something of the same sort here! And I was very apprehensive, for it was a new experience to me.

Next they prayed for guidance about how to continue. After a while, John said, 'I think that there was an operation, connected with isolation. We should pray about it.'

I couldn't think what he meant at first, but at the mention of the word 'isolation' I was suddenly aware of something inside me — an intense, unbearable sorrow. Then I remembered.

'When I was a small child I had a bone abscess, and I was in hospital. I was isolated behind glass because of suspected tuberculosis. I think that started my fear of isolation.'

So they prayed for release from the sadness of that isolation which had scarred me, and asked God to come into that part of my life.

One of them must have sensed how I was feeling: 'Just relax. If you want to say something, say it. If you want to cry, just cry. Just do what you want. Feel free to stand up, or walk around, or anything.'

I started sobbing, and sobbed for ages. I have never sobbed like that before or since, and throughout my sobbing they just went on praying. The feeling I had then was the same as I'd had in church, but to a greater degree. Then quite suddenly it went, and my sobbing just stopped. It just stopped; there was nothing gradual about it as there is when one is unhappy or upset.

At that point they said a prayer, closing the session and sealing it with God's Holy Spirit. They said that they would stop praying with me for that day.

'We're going to get something to eat,' Mary said. 'Would you like to come with us or would you rather just stay here?'

I stayed there, feeling a sort of calm, but at the same time puzzled that so much was happening to me. I was wondering why, when so much had taken place, I didn't feel a lot better. The daily routine of my normal life seemed very remote and far away. I was becoming engrossed in the whole process of what was going on. It was all rather bewildering.

32

BATTLE FOR RELEASE

That night I had a dream. I saw a country lane with a lot of dust, and a cart and an Indian woman. I couldn't see myself, but I knew that I was there and that I was frightened. The woman got very angry, because I was on a different path or lane from her, and yet I was with her. She kept babbling on in some local dialect which I couldn't understand, getting more and more angry.

I woke up completely perplexed, for the dream seemed to be totally out of character. I'd never before dreamed of coloured people, or of people talking in other languages. It slowly dawned on me that it might have been an implanted dream, and I was bothered by it.

I got up and dressed and went downstairs. Nobody else was up, so I made myself some coffee, and sat in the kitchen praying. I wasn't sure whether or not to tell John and Mary about my dream. As I couldn't see the significance of it, I told myself that perhaps I was being fanciful. After all, people do dream strange things.

Then I began to feel physically unwell and thought that I would just go back to bed and stay there. But they'd said that they were intending to pray with me that morning, so I decided that I shouldn't delay things. I went upstairs, made my bed, and by the time I got down again, everyone else was having breakfast. Afterwards, I played with the children for a while, then John came and told me that they were not going to pray with me that morning after all, as they felt they needed to pray on their own about it first.

I'd had enough! I thought I might as well go straight back home! But I couldn't do that for I had to recognize that God was working in my life — that was what held me there. I felt ill — emotionally drained. I did nothing all day, just lazed about, went for a walk, sat in the garden.

That evening there was a meeting in the house attended by lots of people. I joined in, but didn't seem to be part of it. I was aware of the joy of those present, and I realized that many who had come to the meeting had had connections with John and Mary and the team through ministry in the past.

Afterwards, I asked John if they would pray with me before I went to bed. I was convinced that they didn't intend to do so, and my dream of the previous night still bothered me. I told him about it, explaining that while it didn't actually sound too unpleasant, it had somehow worried me.

'People often have dreams which can be relevant to what the Lord is doing,' he said.

'Oh, I'm probably just making a fuss about nothing,' I replied, minimizing it all.

'Before we go up, we'll pray for God's protection over the whole household,' John assured me.

I slept well that night. But when I woke up the next morning there was a strong taste of curry in my mouth. I went to the bathroom and cleaned my teeth twice, but the taste persisted. I couldn't understand it. I hadn't eaten anything, and there had certainly not been any curry in the house anyway. I didn't eat breakfast, and the taste became stronger and my skin felt coarse. I looked in the mirror — I was very pale.

After breakfast John and Mary went into the sitting-room, saying that they were going to pray. The phone rang. Someone apparently wanted Mary to go out somewhere, for she came back into the room asking, 'Will it be all right if I go?'

John said firmly, 'No. I think that we should both pray with Liesl.'

I was very embarrassed that they might smell the curry, but they didn't say anything about it. I wondered what they were going to pray about, as I felt that in some way I had to keep tabs on what was happening. I couldn't help remembering the man in the room next door on the day after my arrival, and I was worried about what would happen if I screeched.

John apologized. 'I'm sorry we didn't see you yesterday,' he said, 'but we're sure that you're going to be a lot more free.'

'I'm a bit nervous this morning,' I admitted.

'Is it about anything in particular?' Mary asked.

'I don't know really. I'm wondering what's going to happen. Will it hinder things if I'm tense and nervous?' I said.

'Just relax and trust God,' they told me. 'He is all-powerful.'

That morning they started by praying for protection, claiming God's power and proclaiming Jesus as Lord. They asked God to guide and lead them. As they did so, the taste of curry increased, and John said that he could smell curry.

'I've been tasting curry all morning, but I haven't eaten anything spicy at all,' I told them.

'Has anything like this ever happened to you before?' John asked.

'No, it hasn't,' I assured them. We were all silent for a while.

Then John said, 'Was there a ceremony, a dedication, a handing-over, perhaps when you were a baby?'

'I don't know.'

Then he asked me, 'Are you a twin?'

'Yes, I am.'

He asked me whether I was the younger twin. When I replied that I was, he said, 'Then you are the baby in the ceremony. You're being given something, a bangle or a necklace, as a symbol. You're being handed over to the local gods.' He paused, then he asked, 'Were you born in India?'

'Yes.'

'Well, it was probably some local custom or ceremony.'

'I'm sure my parents would never have been involved in anything like that,' I protested.

'It's possible that it might have been quite an innocent ceremony, and those taking part wouldn't necessarily have realized that there was a spiritual danger. It's rather like ouija boards and fortune telling. People usually have no intention of invoking satanic power, but an opening can be created.'

They prayed again. Now I felt a blackness, an awareness of blackness. I was quite detached, whereas when they talked about the ceremony I'd felt chaos, spiritual chaos — every emotion, every sensation, all at once and quite indistinguishable.

John told me that they were now dealing with an evil spirit connected with death.

'A curse was put on you at the time of that ceremony,' he said.

They continued praying for a long time. While they were praying, I felt a great struggle within me. I sensed the power of God drawing out something which was deep inside, but at the same time I was aware of a strong resistance.

After a while John asked the spirit to name itself, saying that its time was up. It didn't respond, so he demanded in the name of Jesus that it identify itself — 'Ulak'.

'Ulak, your time is up. The power of God has revealed you. You have no place in this woman. We come before you with the sword of the Spirit and the power of the blood of Christ, and we command you to come out of her, now, in the name of Jesus.'

For a moment, a split second, I felt like a totally different person. The taste of curry was extremely strong, and my skin texture became coarser. Then I was aware of a great sense of exhaustion, and I knew something traumatic had taken place, though I didn't understand quite what. I was still in the same room, in the same chair, and John and Mary hadn't changed, but something very deep had happened.

I was amazed that God had shown them so much about me — about things I knew nothing of at the time.

For quite a while I just sat there silently while they talked over the whole situation, saying again and again that it was incredible what God had done. They were sure that he must have had his hand on me all through my life. They explained that I had been under a curse of death, and because Satan had had a hold on me for so long, he would not give up easily. They felt that further prayer was needed for other problems.

'But there is nothing to fear, for God is stronger,' they reassured me.

'I understand that, but why do I feel so physically ill?' I asked.

'I am not at all surprised,' John answered.

'You've had deep ministry.'

I was exhausted and went to bed, sleeping till the following morning.

33

THE LAST STRONGHOLD

I spent the next day quietly. The house was a happy place, full of fun and laughter, with a very honest and uncritical atmosphere, a united household. As well as being home for a number of people, it was used as a healing and counselling centre. It had been furnished attractively in a practical sort of way. Everything was sensible and well cared for.

John did carpentry in his spare time and Jackie, his wife, who was very shy and gentle, looked after the house and the cooking. She was very patient, never apparently put out when people weren't there to eat the meals she'd prepared, when the ministry had gone on through recognized mealtimes. There were several other people who came and went, members of the team, but I had nothing to do with them directly so I didn't get to know them.

When I woke up the following morning I had a strange sensation. My head felt as if it had been put on ice. The feeling came in waves, and it felt as though cold water was dripping onto the top of my head. I told them that I was feeling rather peculiar, and I didn't understand why. Surely I ought to be better now? They tried to explain, but somehow I wasn't able to follow. They said they felt that more prayer was necessary.

It was then that I found that I could be totally

trusting in their faith. Until that time I'd felt that I had to involve my own faith with what was happening. Suddenly I was glad that I'd gone there, and had stayed. I now felt free to tell them that I'd been involved with drugs, and explain more about my life.

As on other occasions, they prayed and read from the Bible. I'd noticed that they always held their Bibles while they were praying. I really could feel the authority of God was with them, and at the end of each session there had been such a calm, such peace, that even when I was apprehensive I had an almost tangible sense of God's presence.

That morning they suggested that I went to my room to pray on my own for a while and they gave me passages from the Bible to read and meditate on. After an hour or so I came downstairs, and we all had a cup of coffee, chatting about what I was feeling, and about the icy sensation in my head. I asked why there should be a need for all this after God had actually healed me.

John explained, 'God often does things in stages, not all at once. He has it under control, and he knows what he is doing.'

Then they came and stood by me. Even before they started praying I had a sensation of great heaviness in my whole body. I remember thinking 'Oh! They haven't even started yet. Whatever is going to happen?'

They spent a long time praising God and thanking him for his goodness, then they prayed with me about my involvement with drugs. They knew that it was a hereditary tie, and with the power of God they broke that tie. It was a battle which left me feeling weak and battered. They continued to pray, claiming for me God's freedom in the area where addiction had been, and praying for his Holy Spirit to fill that area.

We had a break and some coffee. John and Mary were so kind, and in some ways so ordinary, but it was undeniable that God worked through them.

After coffee, John continued praying, asking God to heal any damage done to my body as a result of drug-taking. He commanded Satan to take his hands off my life, and proclaimed that the curse of death was no longer on me. All this was said in a very matter-of-fact way. Then he prayed against the spirit of infirmity, and I remember thinking 'Oh, that would explain why I've had so much sickness'.

My body still felt incredibly heavy. It was then that John asked me, 'Have you ever dabbled in witchcraft or palmistry or the occult?'

I told him about the palmistry and about my interest in horoscopes. I did somehow know that these things were wrong in God's eyes and John confirmed it, quoting a passage from the Bible, from the book of Deuteronomy, chapter 18, verse 10. He explained that these things were not only wrong, but dangerous.

'Do you still read palms?' he asked. 'Can you give me an instance of your readings coming true?'

So I told him about the incident with Lyn and the death of her father.

Again he asked, 'Do you still do it?'

'No, but I do find that I'm drawn to it,' I admitted.

'Have you renounced it before the Lord?'

'No, I haven't.'

'I do feel that you should do that now,' he suggested.

So I prayed, asking for forgiveness. Then they

prayed. They told me that the sins of parents are passed on, and that this involvement with palmistry was hereditary from my mother's side of the family. I told them then about my mother and grandmother and their interest in palmistry and suchlike. Then they started to pray asking God to break that tie.

At that, my arms from the elbows down became unbearably heavy. They carried on praying.

I cried out, 'Oh, my arms!' but still they went on, and the more they prayed, the worse my arms got. I had to grit my teeth; I just couldn't bear it. I tried to lift my arms, but couldn't move. As the praying continued, I said through gritted teeth, 'I can't stand it any more. Stop praying.'

Mary said, 'We will stop if you really want that, but we feel that we ought to go on. God is with us.' I felt reassured by her words.

I could not move my hands at all. I thought that perhaps I could use one hand to lift the other, but I couldn't move even a finger. As I looked at them, they started to darken until they were completely black, at the same time becoming stiff and distorted. It was frightening, and the heaviness became absolutely unbearable.

John asked me then to proclaim Jesus as Lord, but I couldn't even ungrit my teeth, much less get the words out. Then suddenly it began to subside, the heaviness slowly went, and the colour returned to normal. The aching left me. I just sat there absolutely amazed.

I asked them if they'd seen the colour of my hands, and whether they'd ever seen anything like it before. They said that they had, just once. I continued to sit there. I felt bowled over, but did feel physically better. I was aware of a tranquillity in the air. With every breath I took, I breathed in peace.

'It is wonderful what God has done in your life,' said John.

'Yes,' confirmed Mary. 'Clearly he has had his hand on you from the beginning. Let's pray now that he will fill all those areas of your being with the Holy Spirit which have been damaged by evil. She was referring to Jesus' teaching, when he described how evil spirits had re-entered the house — or person — which had been swept clean but left empty.

They prayed for me. And then I prayed that God would use me in his kingdom. Afterwards I said that I was worried that I might not be sure when God was using me. There was silence for a while. Then Mary said, 'Wait and see. God will unfold it, in his own time.'

I was still very puzzled by all that had happened to me. I spent the rest of that day thinking about the events of the whole week, almost unable to believe it or to take it in. I realized that I'd had a rather unusual experience, and that I'd probably have, on occasion, to explain it to others, so I asked Mary and John a number of questions. I still found it hard to accept that it had been possible for me to be possessed and to be a Christian at the same time.

'And why didn't this all happen when I was healed?' I asked. 'Surely when God met me, he must also have met the power of evil which was in me, and his presence in my life would have cast out the evil?'

'Jesus always comes into a person's life when he is asked in,' John explained. 'And then sometimes he works on further problems from within. He often deals with us in layers, at the right time for us. It may have been that there were certain areas of your life which Jesus hadn't previously gone into. He started the work in you with your healing, and this now is part of a continuing process. He always deals with us individually, at his own pace.'

Mary added, 'We're quite sure that you are, and were, a Christian. In fact, we never minister in this way to people who are not Christians — it would be too dangerous. This sort of ministry has been neglected in church life and teaching; there are so many people with problems who need God's help, and we feel that it should be brought out into the open more. It's so sad to see people struggling with difficulties and looking for help from psycho-therapy and tranquillizers instead of through the church, but demon and spirit possession just don't seem to be acceptable doctrine in most churches today. Even Christians who read the Bible regu-larly and carefully seem to overlook the fact that again and again Jesus healed the sick *and* cast out evil spirits. They can accept the first as being relevant today, but not the second. In fact, even though you had experienced his healing, you were rather like that yourself when you came here, weren't you, Liesl?

'And really there's nothing to be frightened of, for after all, God is more powerful, and all Christians know and accept that. And Jesus is the same yesterday, today and for ever — and so is his work. As he says in the Gospels, "I am telling you the truth; whoever believes in me will do what I do".'

I recently discussed this point with Mary again, and she repeated that they believe it is always right to pray for the sick, whether Christians or not. God will bless the sick person even if he or she is not healed. And the other thing she said was, 'Jesus commanded us to pray — so pray!'

But she underlined again that she and her group would never minister in the area of deliverance to anyone who was not a Christian. She warned me that there are misguided people who dabble in this area while lacking power and faith in Jesus.

'That is why we have described it as a dangerous ministry,' she said.

So after my week with them I went back home. Outwardly perhaps I seemed little different. But inwardly I was released from the bond of fear and sadness which I've tried to describe, and now I had some understanding of the 'death-wish' of my hospital days.

How can I explain how I felt?

From the time of my healing and conversion I'd had an awareness of Jesus' presence in my life, of his joy and his peace. I had been deeply conscious of my commitment to him, and confident that he had an overall plan for my life.

But now I knew a freedom, a cleanness, a wholeness, a security that went further. His touch and his power had converted the bondage of fear, panic and sadness into joy, and into knowledge that he could reach into any pit, however deep.

He moved me into a new realm of awareness of his presence. I knew that whatever might happen to me, he would be in charge, he would protect me and his peace would be with me.

I had a new hope and excitement in life, and now that my internal struggles had ceased, I was free to express that excitement. My experience convinced me beyond any possible doubt that Satan actually exists, and that the Christian life is, in part, a personal battle against him.

Knowing one's enemy, and knowing of his certain defeat through the power of prayer, is exhilarating. I was free to serve God, and to share in his victory.

POSTSCRIPT

Writing all this down has been extremely difficult and painful, but I've known for a long time that the story had to be told.

I remember the first time I did tell it to a large group of people. James had urged me to do so, believing that I should. But I was very reluctant. In fact I was adamant at first that I would not. For how could I ever face those looks of shock and incredulity from friends and neighbours who knew me simply as Liesl, the vicar's wife, mother of Emily and Iona?

But James persisted. So I went for a long early morning walk, thinking about the matter, and wondering what I ought to do. I opened the Bible at random, challenging God to give me the answer. I read a verse from the twenty-second Psalm, 'I will praise you to all my brethren. I will stand up before the congregation and testify of the wonderful things you have done.'

So I spoke at that meeting. It was nerve-wracking, agony, but I hoped that after that it might become easier to write it down. I'm not sure it's worked out that way. Baring one's soul — laying out for public inspection one's madness and one's memories — is an awesome business.

But the power of God is infinitely more awesome, and it was by his power that I was restored to normality. My need was great, and he met it. He still meets my needs today, for my healing, my encounter with Jesus, my deliverance from evil were not isolated events but part of God's overall plan for my life. He placed me in a position where I could choose to follow him. I'm grateful that I made that choice, that I can know the joy, the peace, as well as the fulfilment and the excitement of the Christian life, for it is beyond comparison.

I have not written this book to entertain or to preach. I just wanted to convey something of my experiences of God's power. For whatever a person's attitude to some of the events and happenings described in this book, the unalterable fact remains that the person who lay on the mattress in that locked room, 'pale, wan, a pathetic sight, oblivious of even the presence of her friends', is now a wife, a mother, and a Christian.

My own life confirms the truth of the words I heard in that church hall: 'God can do anything, absolutely anything.'

HELL'S ANGEL
Brian Greenaway with Brian Kellock

Brian Greenaway was president of a Hell's Angel chapter. He was violent, full of hate, deeply into drugs.

Then, in Dartmoor Prison, he had an experience which changed him completely.

This is Brian's own story – powerful, sometimes ugly but real. It describes his tough early years, his dramatic conversion and his struggles to work out a new way of life.

COPING WITH DEPRESSION
Myra Chave-Jones

'Depression is as universal as the common cold. It can be so slight as to be hardly worth the name – just a passing mood which will be gone tomorrow. It can be a vague feeling of persistent dreariness that takes the sparkle out of life as we carry on with the usual routine. Or, at the other extreme, it can almost totally paralyse action . . .'

What causes depression? How can we recognize it, in ourselves and in others? And what help is available? Myra Chave-Jones is a practising psychotherapist and a Christian. She writes with a deep understanding and sympathy for those living under the dark shadow of depression – isolated and helpless – for whom it seems 'always winter and never Christmas'. Her book is full of clear information and practical examples.

She writes not only for those suffering depression, but also for all who live close to them. She describes what depression feels like, the treatments, those who may be specially at risk. She deals with the factors of guilt and religious doubt. She also offers constructive help in handling depression and in avoiding its recurrence.

HOSTAGE
Fausto Bucheli with Robin Maxson

It was Fausto Bucheli's last day in San Salvador – or so he thought. Tomorrow he would be returning to his wife and family. This afternoon there was no need to take the back route. Things were calm in the city.

Suddenly a jeep pulled out in front and jammed on its brakes. A truck hit their van from behind. They were trapped. Armed terrorists leaped from the jeep. The sound of gunfire filled the air. 'This is a kidnapping,' one of them shouted.

For American businessman Fausto Bucheli forty-seven days of terror had just begun. Humiliated and in agony he was imprisoned in a filthy cell, never knowing if he would live to see another day.

This tense, real-life story is the account of his terrible ordeal and that of his family, and of the high-powered negotiations for his release. It is the story of a man who reached the depths of despair – and in that solitary cell found real freedom.